# Freshwater Fishing
## in Australia

# Freshwater Fishing
## in Australia

## Gordon Wood

REED

# DEDICATION

*For the long line of fishing freaks it has been my pleasure to associate with over the·years, both in England and Australia. But especially for my father and his father, my brother Paul, Ernie Daniels, Raymond Wines, Bernard Alfrey and 'Smithy' wherever he may be. And for the late Peter Mead, without whose prompting I may never have written this book.*

REED BOOKS PTY LTD
2 Aquatic Drive Frenchs Forest NSW 2086

*First published 1982*
*Revised and reprinted 1989*

© Gordon Wood 1982

National Library of Australia
Cataloguing-in-Publication Data:
Wood, Gordon.
    Freshwater fishing in Australia.

    Includes index.
    ISBN 0 7301 0279 3

    1. Fishing — Australia. 2. Fishes, Fresh-water —
Australia. I. Title.

799.1'1'0994

*Set in 9/10 Helvetica by B&D Modgraphic, Adelaide*
*Printed and bound in Singapore through Imago Productions (F.E.) Pte Ltd*

# CONTENTS

# INTRODUCTION

This is a fishing book, describing in some detail most of the major freshwater fishing areas throughout Australia. And yet it's just a little more. Within its pages are occasionally mentioned places of interest near the centre of the fishing scene that those on holiday may wish to visit while giving both the fish and fishing a breather. The first time I ever fished the Eildon area of Victoria, for example, I was disappointed to learn later that the Snobs Creek Hatchery was close by, and that I'd missed the opportunity of paying it a visit.

Eventually I made good this mistake. But so that can never happen to you, the hatchery is mentioned in the section dealing with the area of Eildon, and hatcheries in other states are also given. The caves throughout the wilderness of Australia are worth inspecting, and many of these are listed also, as are various national parks, and other places worthy of the visitor's interest. Most are in one way or another connected with fishing, but not all.

The Southern Cloud Park located on the Snowy Mountains Highway, for example, has nothing to do with fishing at all. But when bound for the Eucumbene, why not make a slight detour to inspect a few remains of the plane that rested quite unsuspected in the Deep Creek area for 27 years? The Japanese War Cemetery at Cowra, New South Wales, is again unconnected with fishing, yet here is a material link with what is believed to be the greatest escape of prisoners-of-war of all time.

The Murray River for much of its length is served by tiny townships, and these too have been listed, where relevant, as possible bases for the angler determined to get a big cod. At the same time, interests away from his sport have been mentioned for the benefit of those in tow. The children at least will appreciate a few hours away from the riverside, and perhaps even dad and mum need a break.

On waters like Lake Pedder, however, we're there with not a single thought on our minds other than the massive trout we hope to encounter as, like men demented, we persevere in the vilest weather to battle with just one of those Pedder giants—and who can think of a better way to burn up energy?

The purpose of all the information contained here is to make this a useful reference from which the angler will not only learn about the existence of a water but will also get to know exactly what he can expect to find there in terms of fish species, their average size, and the lures, baits and flies on which to take them. Don't forget that it is the fisherman's responsibility to check when seasons are open and closed, as these vary from state to state and water to water. When live bait is allowed to be used, and what sort, is also to be checked on. For instance, legislation concerning the use of frogs as bait is changing, so although frogs might be suggested in a chapter in this book, the law might well have altered since the writing of the chapter. So always enquire first.

Available accommodation in most areas is given; this information has been restricted mainly to caravan and camping parks to help cut the cost of a visit. Included is the availability of on-site vans, which more anglers are now turning to in preference to a tent. Facts about the admittance or otherwise of pets is unnecessary information to those who haven't any, but many anglers fish with their pets alongside them, and the first question they ask when booking in at a caravan park is whether or not their dog is allowed also. I know, having been turned away from many such parks because of my four-legged friend.

To help the angler further a list of State Government Tourist Bureaux and Travel Centres has also been included, so use it to the full when contemplating an angling trip that is a little out of your normal fishing area.

**NEW SOUTH WALES AND AUSTRALIAN CAPITAL TERRITORY**

# NEW SOUTH WALES
# AND
# AUSTRALIAN CAPITAL TERRITORY

Probably New South Wales can boast of having more anglers than any other state. Most of them will be beach, bay or rock fishermen, but that still leaves a formidable number who concentrate on fishing the freshwater rivers and dams. Almost without exception they'll be trout anglers (a small minority prefer to seek the Murray species), and whenever opportunity allows, many will head for the high country in the Snowy Mountains, where some of the finest trouting of all can be had.

Yet there are many lesser regions where the fishing is good but rarely publicised. The Orana district, for example, is kept shrouded in mystery. If any news leaks out at all about the district, it is to sing the praises of its glorious landscapes—with rarely a word of the fishing at all. Perhaps there is a conspiracy to keep the fishing potential a secret. If that's the case, just think how great it must be!

When dealing with the vast expanse of New South Wales, it is more convenient to cover this state by sections. The Snowy, of course, is well known—but not so the other districts it seems. The fishing in the Hunter region appears to be virtually untapped. Lake Glenbawn, for instance, has a great deal to offer, and the streams provide a good bit of fishing too. So why not give them a go for a change?

The Central Western District also warrants a visit. The trout in the streams may not be monsters, but there are plenty. And while there, why not take time out to inspect some of the caves? The area is riddled with them. Indeed, there's so much to see that unless the angler imposes a bit of self-discipline, he'll end up doing more sightseeing than fishing.

But that's the risk you take when entering any of the districts in New South Wales, for there is always something along the way to persuade you to linger. Watch the rainbows trying to leap the Norfolk Falls in the Warung State Forest of the Orana region, or perhaps call in at the Inland Fisheries Research Station near Narrandera in the Riverina. And what about that monster Murray cod at the hatchery near Wagga Wagga?

Perhaps nowhere else in Australia can the angler so successfully combine his fishing with a bit of sightseeing. Rich in the dastardly deeds of bushrangers, and also in Aboriginal legends, there are so many attractions in New South Wales—and so little time to fit them in as we work our wands along the trout streams.

A little compromising may gain us the best of both worlds. More attention to our itinerary when leaving on an inland fishing trip will allow us to see more in our travels; otherwise whatever we do discover will be by mere chance. And if we were to approach our fishing in such a thoughtless manner we wouldn't catch too many.

But with a little extra planning we can perhaps take a detour or two, to add a bit more depth to our journey. And if a camera is kept cocked, the photographs taken will make a nice change from pictures of fish.

## CENTRAL WESTERN DISTRICT

More gold than fish appears to have been taken from the rivers and streams covered in this section, but that was some time ago. Today the pay-off is more likely to be in the form of some of the nice trout to be taken from the rivers and dams—Lake Canobolas and Lake Cargelligo to mention two.

This region of New South Wales starts at the western slopes of the Blue Mountains and continues to Lake Cargelligo, a distance of about 400 kilometres, and is roughly half-way from the coast to the South Australian border. Here the country is wild and woolly enough for us to be envious of the pathfinders who first left their tracks here, to open the terrain to the world.

We can return to those days by visiting the Lachlan Vintage Village at Forbes, where a re-creation of the gold-rush days awaits us. Many early goldmining regions have been preserved, and doubtless some still provide a few grains of gold-dust, but hardly enough to start the mad stampede off all over again.

But it is the creeks, rivers, lakes and dams which bring us to the area, for we know that wherever we are in New South Wales, the trout fishing won't be far away. Here then are just a few of the waters to be found in the Central Western District, along with other places of interest, such as caves, which add much to a fleeting trip to the area. There are also a number of festivals taking place at various times of the year throughout the region.

### LAKES AND DAMS

#### Lake Canobolas

Fifty million years ago, the mountain of Canobolas was a volcano, but at the bottom of it today lies Lake Canobolas, a popular fishing centre. Situated 8 km south-west of Orange via the Cargo Road, the lake is part of a park setting spread over 80 hectares. Within the park is a scout camp and camping area, a 10-hectare deer enclosure containing a herd of fallow deer, and also a park geared to family outings. The Apex Play Park is equipped with barbecues, a children's play area and a collection of shallow ponds. Although no power boating is permitted, there's a suitable ramp for other types of vessels on the western shore. Safe swimming areas have been allocated and in season pedal boats may be used to add to the fun. Trout fishing is said to be extremely good here during the open season (October to March), and all things being equal a splendid time should be had by those paying the water a call. Near the lake there is a camping area with all the usual facilities.

#### Mount Canobolas Park

Within the area of the lake is also a 1500-hectare sanctuary for Australian flora and fauna. There are many paths for those who wish to walk through some breathtaking scenery, and a detailed map showing the best tracks to wander along can be obtained from the Orange Visitors Centre. The Federal Falls is particularly recommended to the visitor. No less than 15 developed picnic areas are there to be used. Mount Canobolas Park is 14 km south-west of Orange along the Canobolas Road.

## Carcoar Dam

Found after a short 9 km drive north-east of Carcoar along the Mid-Western Highway, Carcoar Dam provides some excellent fishing at times. But as with most huge areas of water, most other aquatic sports are practised here, which is apt to spoil the fishing a bit. But as always, if we persevere, we'll win in the end. The dam provides the water necessary for the irrigation of the Belubula Valley. There are camping facilities close to the dam, and nearby we find the historic village of Carcoar, where the first bank robbery in Australian history took place in 1863. Members of Ben Hall's gang were the culprits, and the bank they robbed still stands today.

## Lake Cargelligo

Swimming, fishing, boating and water-skiing—it all takes place on this lake, near the town bearing the same name. The lake is controlled by the Water Resources Commission, and is a refuge for birds and animals. It would be a very dull angler who didn't pause in his fishing to admire the wild birds around him—black swans, pelicans, wild ducks and geese. But more interesting must be the members of the parrot family that abound here. Wee jugglers and galahs, white cockatoos, kookaburras, pigeons, eagles—all add their grace and colour to the scene, so don't go to Lake Cargelligo without a camera.

## Wyangala Dam

This huge dam is situated on the Lachlan River, and can be reached by driving 40 km south-east of Cowra along the excellent Wyangala Dam Road. From the south one travels via Goulburn and Bigga.

The Wyangala Dam is an exceptionally large and beautiful water, containing a good selection of fish, including brown and rainbow trout, catfish, golden and silver perch and also a fair head of Macquarie perch, plus carp and a sprinkling of redfin. The odd Murray cod may also be had.

Below the dam in a most picturesque setting the Lachlan River sweeps over the rocks and past the willows that so characterise the area. Fishing immediately below the dam is not permitted, but further downstream you might see some entertaining rainbows.

Night fishing at Wyangala produces large catches of catfish at times, taken on grubs, worms or dead fish. A few extra large trout may also appear, making the effort of fishing at night more than worthwhile. This dam, like so many, also caters for those with an interest beyond their rod-tips. Water-skiing at times attracts a lot of followers here, as do sailing and swimming, camping and hiking; but generally there's room enough for everyone.

Boating is permitted on the lake, but permission must first be sought from the park ranger, who will then pass on to the boat-owner regulations which must be followed. At the same time it may be a good idea to ask about the fishing. There is deep water in the dam, with some sheltered areas, but upstream proceed with caution, because tree growth can be a hazard.

## TROUT STREAMS

Within this area are many fine trout streams that deserve some attention. From Cox's River, close to the Jenolan Caves Road, for example, there are often some decent trout to be had. But the fishing is usually a little better in the River Kowmung, which rises in the vicinity of the Tuglow Caves and then passes beneath the Kanangra Walls to meet the Cox's River in the gorge near Jenolan. Many nice fish are taken from the Oberon area, where the big dam and adjacent streams keep the angler busy. There are also trout in Sodwalls Creek, which can be reached from the township with the same name by travelling along the road from Rydal to Tarana.

The big Ben Chifley Dam in the region of Bathurst offers some very fine trout fishing, often done from a boat. But on Oberon Dam there is a ban on boats going on the water. Molong Creek in the Orange area is also worth fishing for trout, as are the headwaters of the Bell River. But to obtain the full benefit of angling in these streams a detailed map of the entire area will put the trout-fisher where the fish are. It should be noted also that some streams within this district are restricted to fly-fishing only, so check this out while seeking whatever local advice is offering, for that's another way to reach the fish quickly.

Many other rivers and streams spread their water all over this territory, and almost without exception they all contain trout—not equal in size to those found in some of the dams perhaps, but big enough to let us know they're on the line and kicking up merry hell as we coax them to the net. The streamlined trout of the streams is a fighter, and no mistake!

## PLACES OF INTEREST

### Abercrombie Caves

These are 72 km south of Bathurst along the Bathurst–Goulburn Road. Smaller but perhaps more beautiful than most, the glowing main feature of the Abercrombie Caves is the Arch Cave (thought to be one of the finest of its kind in the world). The Arch Cave is enormous in comparison to the other caves in this network—221 metres long, 60 metres wide, and in parts over 30 metres high. Other smaller caves include the Bushrangers' Cave, where the legendary Ben Hall hid out, the Hall of Terpsichore, featuring a man-made stage, the Cathedral and the Grove Cave, a smaller but far prettier grotto near the main cavern. In the bad old days outlaws by the dozen apparently used the caves as a refuge.

### Bathurst Gold Diggings

Established at Karingal Village on Mount Panorama, from which there's a fine view. Here is reconstructed all the paraphernalia associated with the goldfields. Much of the machinery used in the old days is still in working condition, and a film show on the subject may be seen at the local information centre at Karingal Village.

### Sir Joseph Banks Nature Reserve

Situated on Mount Panorama, the reserve consists of 41 hectares of rugged bushland offering some magnificent scenery. Wildlife of many kinds roams freely, including wallabies, kangaroos and koalas. Organised tours and mini-bus trips around the reserve can be arranged through the Tourist Bureau in the Civic Centre at Bathurst.

**Japanese War Cemetery**
Five kilometres north of Cowra alongside the Cowra–Canowindra Road is a sad reminder of the Second World War. The cemetery contains the remains of 247 Japanese prisoners-of-war who died while taking part in the mass breakout from the prisoner-of-war encampment at nearby Cowra on 4 August 1944. Another 275 Japanese servicemen and civilians who were held captive in other parts of Australia are buried here too. The cemetery contains examples of traditional Japanese landscaping and architecture. Four Australian soldiers died here also, and an Australian war cemetery is adjacent to the Japanese one. Two kilometres south-east is the actual site of the escape, where a plaque on a memorial gives an account of the event.

**Jenolan Caves**
Located 45 km south-west of Hartley by the Hampton Road, the Jenolan Caves are more widely known than others in the Central Western District. More than three million visitors have been entertained by the glittering beauty of the Jenolan Caves since they were opened to the public a hundred years ago. Set in the surrounding scenery of a vast nature reserve, the region of the caves is a delightful place for a holiday.

## THE HUNTER DISTRICT

This district takes its name from the Hunter River, which rises in the Mount Royal Range and then heads westwards, before twisting south on its journey to Glenbawn Dam, then south-east through the sprawling Hunter Plain. The landscape of this district has been changed rather more than most by man, its terrain having been well farmed over the years. Yet it's pleasant country for all that, with hilly eucalypt forests. Ferns, mosses, lichens and fungi also abound in the cool, damp climate.

The area begins north of Sydney at Catherine Hill Bay, extending a further 145 kilometres north to Tuncurry, and stretches 275 kilometres west to the Great Dividing Range. Much of the region is coastal and the twin resorts of Forster and Tuncurry are popular with those taking part in aquatic sports in salt water. Inland there is trout fishing, in man-made waters like Lostock, Liddell, Chichester and Glenbawn dams, and in the rivers, with trout that oblige us on bait, fly and spinner.

There are, however, other attractions to distract our fanatical urges whenever we are at the edge of a lake, river or stream. It is at times better to surrender for a while to whatever beckons us away from the water, for we will return more determined than ever. We'll look at the water anew, approach it perhaps from a different angle, and who knows? Perhaps success will then be ours. So never despair when called away to collect further supplies—it may well be a blessing in disguise.

### LAKES AND DAMS

**Lake Glenbawn**
Situated on the upper reaches of the Hunter River the Glenbawn Dam was completed in 1958. A popular tourist venue, the dam provides water for irrigation, and also acts as a storage for flood mitigation. Referred to sometimes as the water playground of the Hunter Valley, Lake Glenbawn is suitable for fishing, swimming, power boating, sailing and water-skiing.

A boat ramp is available on the eastern shore, and picnic and barbecue facilities are found at various points around the lake. Smaller boats (under 10 hp) may be launched from the roadway adjacent to Apex Park. There is accommodation in two holiday cabins, each able to house six persons. A modern caravan park and camping area offer all the usual amenities expected these days. Enquire locally about the fishing.

### Lake Liddell
Located 26 km north-west of Singleton, 14 km south of Muswellbrook, Lake Liddell was built to provide pondage for the Liddell power station. Suitably situated, the lake and foreshores offer a delightful setting for aquatic fun, including the kind that interests us most.

### Lostock Dam
A fairly open water situated 19 km north-west of Gresford, on the Paterson River, and reached by the Lostock Road. Restrictions on water sports may deter a few, but boating is permitted, with an 8-knot speed limit. A permit to launch craft must be obtained from the officer-in-charge of the dam. Swimming and fishing are allowed, and there are excellent picnic facilities and a well organised caravan park.

## THE STREAMS
The plateau country of the Barrington Tops and the adjoining Gloucester Tops is the source of many rivers, among them the Barrington, Williams, Allyn, Kerripit, Chichester and Paterson. The Allyn River is especially popular with tourists, with its picnic and barbecue areas and camping sites. Such an area can be reached by travelling 45 km north of Gresford and 45 km north-west of Dungog, where there are many access tracks for the angler's convenience. Fishing is done in pools reached by walking along the tracks by the river. Seek local advice about how to tempt a few fish, but if that isn't forthcoming, stick to tried and proven methods associated with other waters. It is a safe bet that one will work.

The Hunter District perhaps doesn't have as many freshwater rivers and dams as other New South Wales districts, but what it does have is scenery. The terrific views will compensate us to a degree.

## PLACES OF INTEREST
### Barrington Tops
An interesting and vast plateau providing the source of a number of rivers. The bushland here is noted for unusual specimens of native plant life, including ferns, staghorns and native orchids. The amazing variety of wildlife includes wallabies and kangaroos, brush turkeys, lyrebirds, and some bronze-winged pigeons. Among the facilities available are picnic and camping areas 60 km north-west of Dungog. Take the access road through Bendolba and Salisbury; or through Gloucester, either along the Barrington Tops Forest Road or the Gloucester Tops Forest Road. It seems an effort but the trip's worth it.

### Nature Wonderland
This is in Louth Park Road, 3 km south-west of Maitland and is just the place to take the kids! There are kangaroos and koalas, wallabies and

emus, birds and reptiles of all sorts to entertain the little ones. There's even a train ride for them. Barbecues available.

## Watagan Mountains

This range is within the span of the Watagan State Forest, and situated roughly 20 km south-east of Cessnock. The rare, rugged natural beauty of the area must be seen to be appreciated. Lookout points are equipped with facilities for a picnic or barbecue—Heaton, Hunter and Flat Rock lookouts are three.

# MURRAY DISTRICT

The grand old Murray River creates a natural border here between the states of Victoria and New South Wales. The border between the latter state and South Australia is also established within this region, while the boundary forging north separates this district from the Riverina and Far Western regions. The area is rich in pastoral and farming land, needing a network of irrigation channels to help keep it so.

From an angling point of view this is the place to be if you're not after the much hallowed trout. It is the fondly termed Murray species that are to be had from the Murray—cod, callop, and the introduced redfin. The sporting shooter, too, will find an interest here, where anything from quail to wild pigs may be encountered, along with wild duck.

Lake Mulwala and the Hume Weir are normally considered as Victorian waters although, since a New South Wales licence is required to fish them, both have been included in this section. Each is fed by the Murray and offer in their own right some first-rate, fishing for warm-water species, and also for the splendid trout both carry. The European carp will be there too, testing the skill of some and the patience of others who loathe the species for surviving in a world in which even the angler is set to wipe it off the face of the earth.

Like most of the country through which the Murray River unhurriedly passes, the Murray District is a delight to behold, the red gums standing proudly to attention at the water's edge adding much to the often breath-taking scenery. The riverside towns, too, contribute to the splendour.

## NATIVE FISH OF THE MURRAY RIVER
### Murray Cod

The species of fish that inhabit the deep placid waters of the Murray River are unique by world standards. The Murray cod, for example, is widely known beyond the shores of Australia, partly because of its great size but mainly because it's so symbolic of the river in which it lives—slow, lazy and mighty big. The Murray cod (Maccullochella peeli) is said to grow to 90 kg, although some anglers believe that it probably grows much bigger, and the Murray River is certainly large enough to hide any number of such monster fish. The Murray cod is found in every state but Tasmania, where the waters are too cold to accommodate it comfortably. First spawning at four years of age, more than 20 000 eggs are produced, but few of the hatched fish appear to develop and survive to old age. Biologists have concluded that this outsize fish eats surprisingly tiny morsels. Crustaceans, and to a lesser degree molluscs and small fish, make up the bulk of its diet, so how it manages to become so big is indeed puzzling.

### Trout Cod

Trout cod (*Maccullochella macquariensis*) are by no means as numerous as they were several decades ago, for like so many of our native fish they are fast disappearing. Confined strictly to the cooler reaches of the Murray River and its tributaries in the south, the trout cod is very much an endangered species. Estimated to reach a weight of 16 kg, the species is sadly lacking in research. Little is known about its breeding habits, for instance, and unless some added protection is given it may well soon become extinct.

### Golden Perch

Commonly known as the callop or yellow-belly, the golden perch (*Macquaria ambigua*) is a big Murray River fish, claimed to reach a maximum 26 kg. More commonly widespread than most Murray species, the golden perch is a firm favourite with anglers, who fish for it with baits and lures. Over the years, the species has been introduced to many of the smaller dams, to which it is most adaptable. Spawning normally occurs in slack water where, with the aid of a rise in its level, ideal conditions exist for the buoyant eggs.

### Silver Perch

The silver perch (*Bidyanus bidyanus*) is smaller than the golden perch, attaining at best a weight of 8 kg. Known also as bream, black and silver bream and bidyan, this fish is encountered in Western Australia, South Australia, Victoria, Queensland and New South Wales. Habitually met by the angler in the Murray River system, it offers him good sport on light gear. The fish requires a rise in the level of the water to be induced to spawn, when up to half a million eggs may be shed by the largest fish. The eggs are semi-buoyant, and will drift down with the stream. The species feeds on small aquatic insects, molluscs, shrimps and plant life. It will swim in a shoal and is occasionally seen near the surface in clear water.

### Macquarie Perch

The Macquarie perch (*Macquaria australasica*) is found in the Murray-Darling system in Victoria, New South Wales and possibly South Australia. Abundant above Burrinjuck and Wyangala dams, it was once just as common above Eildon Reservoir but is now something of a rarity there. It spawns during October to November in swiftly running water over a bed of gravel to which the eggs adhere. Said to reach a weight of 4 kg, the Macquarie perch feeds a great deal on insects and their larvae, and responds heartily to fly, bait or spinner. It is reluctant to breed in small ponds, and despite its apparent abundance at the moment, is in danger of becoming extinct.

### Catfish

The freshwater catfish (*Tandanus tandanus*), grows to about 7 kg, and is a fearsome looking creature on the end of a line. Caught in the Murray River and tributaries, except those in the south, this fish spawns in late spring or summer. The eggs are deposited in a circular nest made in the gravel, in which they are guarded and fanned by the male fish. The freshwater catfish appears to be more at home in still-water lakes and in the sluggish flow of backwaters, rather than in a fast moving current, and is very much a bottom feeder, relying mainly on molluscs and crustaceans. Its skin is smooth to the touch and yet very tough, without any scales, which makes it something of an oddity. When feeding it tends to stir up the bottom to create some muddiness of the water. It will accept pieces of meat or dead fish as bait.

## FISHING TECHNIQUES FOR THE MURRAY

Most anglers fishing the Murray dream of getting stuck into a monster Murray cod. Although nowhere nearly as common as they were, big Murray cod are still available for those prepared to study their quarry, learn all they can about it and then set off in pursuit in command of all the facts. What kind of bottom does it prefer; at what time does it normally start feeding; does it inhabit fast water or slow; and most importantly of all, where is it most likely to be found on the Murray? These and other pertinent questions must be asked by the angler in search of big fish of any kind—it's all part of his preparation. To obtain the necessary answers he must then read all he can on his subject—not just stories of good fish taken, although they may of course give him some information, but a complete and thorough study of the species' characteristics also so he may learn about its lifestyle, its feeding habits, and when, where and how it breeds. He is then ready perhaps to set out after his adversary with every hope of success.

He will discover, for instance, that Murray cod are mainly nocturnal fish, and that they're more than contented in deep snaggy holes close to the water's edge. The snaggier the edge, the better cod like it, in fact, especially when the water's barely disturbed by the flow, so here's the kind of place to begin the search. Should some shallower water be nearby, in which frolic little fish, so much the better; the cod won't have far to travel for a feed. So offer as bait the kind of morsel it will be accustomed to, in this case a tiny live fish.

Don't be impatient. Because nothing has yet touched the bait doesn't necessarily mean it never will. Even the smaller cod are quite big fish, and will feed in deadly earnest when in the mood, probably filling themselves to the gills with food before dropping off again into slumber to digest with ease the fruits of their labour.

Obviously, if we want to skull-drag them out of their retreats, then we'll need lines like hawsers that will give us no sport at all. A better idea by far is to locate a comparatively snag-free swim away from the tangled mass of tree-roots beneath which we suspect a big cod is hiding, and to concentrate instead on luring it into open water. Once out of its lair we'll have more than a fighting chance of beating it on a more sensible line.

Some anglers, to their shame, have been known to kill all kinds of birds for bait, because when particularly hungry a big cod will take almost anything—from a live frog or dead mouse to a whopping great water-rat cruising on the top.

Apart from the Murray River and tributaries, good cod are also to be found in many dams, and have also been introduced into the Richmond and Clarence rivers of New South Wales and the Dawson and Mary rivers of Queensland. Thanks to this relatively new stocking programme of Murray cod, that dream for many shouldn't be too far away, but there isn't anything quite like getting one out of the Murray.

Cod trout tactics are the same as those applicable to the Murray cod and, for years in fact, the two fish were said to be one and the same species, so alike are they in appearance and characteristics, although the cod trout is very much on the way out. To catch one these days is something of an achievement. The golden perch, yellow-belly or callop (call it what you will), is, however, far more plentiful, and enjoying immense popularity. Although a giant of 22.7 kg has been recorded, the average fish the angler will catch will weigh no more than a kilo or two. Widespread to areas far beyond the reaches of the Murray, where they've been successfully established, the golden perch is essentially carnivorous, relying on crustaceans and the small forage fish that our spinners represent.

Being mainly bottom feeders, however, they're more likely to be taken on a bait than a lure. A shrimp suspended below a float near the bottom is an accepted method of fooling them into taking the bait. Doubtless a worm jiggled about at the same depth would also be noticed and taken. Many anglers insist on spin-fishing, even when the odds against them are great. In this case, however, the perch will oblige, provided the lure is near the bottom and not worked too fast. Small spoons are preferable, such as the celta and similar, which have rotating blades, though some of the smaller plugs might work just as well.

Fishing for catfish is akin to fishing for eels. Both are prepared to feed at night more so than during the day. Each haunts the sluggish water of backstreams and dams—and both enjoy with relish a dead fish, frog, or similar small creature. The sport offered by the catfish isn't so thrilling, because like most of the warm-water species of the Murray River, they're not exactly built for speed, and therefore depend mainly on sheer weight to make their protest on the end of a line; and if they haven't got that, well . . . there's not much else going for them as sporting fish, though they taste well enough on a plate. The catfish we are familiar with is merely one of more than a thousand different species throughout the world, and most live in freshwater. To catch a cattie in a placid pool, a bait is best fished right on the bottom with just the tiniest sinker, if one must be used at all.

Angling techniques for silver perch are much the same as those recommended for its more regal brother the golden perch, although perhaps a wider range of baits may interest it. Also to be taken at times on trout flies, like the Mrs Simpson and the fuzzy wuzzy, the silver perch is more likely to give a good account of itself when hooked than most other Murray fish, and is therefore more constantly sought in areas where it still congregates in reasonable numbers.

The Macquarie perch, last of the perches to interest us, is something of a black sheep of the extensive perch family—the skeleton in the cupboard if you like—always being confused with the other perch species and never being recognised in its own right. Yet it's more of a sporting fish than the others, likened to its cousin the bass. Indeed, some believe it to be the finest fighter in the south. Susceptible to a fly on the top, the Macquarie perch makes a nice substitute for trout in areas where there are none of these, and the wet flies also make a killing. A useful technique is to drift a mudeye or stonefly nymph near the bottom of the pools these perch inhabit. But the spin-fisher is there too, trying for them with tiny spinners. The bait-fisher is advised to present them with small natural baits, such as worms, mudeyes, and shrimps.

## LAKES AND DAMS

### Hume Reservoir

The Hume Reservoir, 322 kilometres from Melbourne, 506 from Sydney, covers an area of 22 670 hectares, reaches a maximum depth of 42 metres at the dam wall and is the home of trout, redfin, and Murray cod. The reservoir exists for the sole purpose of stabilising the flow of the Murray River, in order to irrigate farming land in New South Wales, Victoria and South Australia—an area of 1 000 000 hectares.

Open to the fisherman throughout the year, this vast water is mainly bait-fished, although angling with a wet fly can be profitable at times, when the level of the dam is rising to flood the grass-carpeted margins. At such times the locals get their fly gear out of mothballs and head for the dam, for past experience has shown this to be the best killing time for trout on the fly-line.

As the water mark gets higher a roving spinner may bring added results, but generally it's the bait-fisher with his assorted goodies who gets into the fish. Situated just 12 km upstream from Albury, the Hume is one of the largest man-made lakes in the country. The roadway over the weir links Victoria with New South Wales, and it is interesting to drive over for the fun of going interstate! Nearby is the Hume Weir Trout Farm, where thousands of rainbow trout are bred commercially. Visitors can prove to themselves that the trout here at least are feeding, by throwing in a handful of food. In fact they're actually encouraged to feed them.

### Mulwala Lake

This very popular water on the Murray River contains mostly redfin growing to about 2 kg or more, which provide some mind-bending sport to the angler appreciating the vast difference between big redfin and little ones. The latter offer easy pickings even to the raw beginner, but the better redfin demand all the native cunning we possess to lure them to a spinner or bait, so cautious are they of our every move.

In this massive, man-made reservoir (also known as Yarrawonga Weir), lives a very good head of Murray cod too, which offers some really excellent fishing at times, though the sport will vary considerably from year to year. Bardi grubs, small live fish and perhaps a large and lively scrubworm are the baits to tempt them, while the lure fancier will work his offering deep and slow, to compensate for the fishes' preference for deep, quiet water where they don't have to battle with the stream to feed.

Mulwala Lake is a relatively shallow sheet of water taking in a vast 4533 hectares, and a New South Wales fishing licence is required to fish in certain areas. Forest and grazing land surround the lake. The township of Mulwala is situated on the northern shore while on the southern shore is the Victorian town of Yarrawonga. The shores are well laid out, and shaded lawns running down to the water's edge make it an ideal place to have a picnic. Many species of birdlife offer a golden opportunity to the wildlife photographer and this huge expanse of water is used for all manner of aquatic pastimes.

It's the fish that beckon us to its shores, however, and quite apart from the two species mentioned above, there are also tench, carp and golden perch to angle for; the last being eagerly sought when the cod fishing is a bit slow. These will fall victim to all kinds of 'meaty' baits, though worms are most often proffered. Spinners, too, will tempt them, if kept near the bed of the lake where golden perch will normally congregate.

Fishing from a boat is the more acceptable method of getting a good bag of fish, but don't feel despondent if you have to fish from the bank. A good many fish will be taken by those marooned there—they just have to try a little harder.

Along with nearby Hume Weir, Mulwala Lake is perhaps the most attractive fishery in the Murray District. Anglers come from many kilometres around to experience the kind of fishing Mulwala has to offer. But if in doubt when arriving on the scene for the first time, seek out the help and advice of those who have obviously been this way before. It is only as we become more accustomed to fishing the water that we may dispense altogether with what others say and do, and concentrate instead on putting a few of our own theories to the test. These might in time prove to be so successful that others will follow our lead.

Yabbies, for example, appear to be the most favoured bait for redfin here, but for better fish something larger and livelier on the hook should bring far better results. So don't become too bogged down with local ideas—try a few of your own.

## MURRAY VALLEY TOWNSHIPS—VICTORIA

### Beechworth
Situated approximately 50 km south-west of Albury is Victoria's most well-preserved goldmining town. Still standing are 32 buildings from the old gold-rush days that are now under the care of the National Trust. The town of Beechworth is also associated with the Kelly gang, and with the adventures of explorer Robert O'Hara Burke, of the Burke and Wills expedition to the Gulf of Carpentaria in 1861.

### Echuca
A well-known riverside township on the Victorian side of the Murray, Echuca is perhaps one of the more popular fishing areas. Even the occasional big trout cod is reported from here, and being nearer to Melbourne than most parts of the Murray, the Victorian will be here to try his luck. A paddle-steamer now operates out of Echuca, to take visitors on a trip back to the heyday of this town when it was a thriving river port.

### Mildura
The city of Mildura is located on the southern bank of the Murray River, and is very much a draw-card for tourists, and takes good care of them so that one day they will return. Ideally situated for those wishing to fish the Murray, the area has more to offer—in particular the paddle-steamers *Melbourne* and *Avoca*, that leave on regular Murray River cruises. One of the country's largest aviaries is also to be seen at the Golden River Fauna Gardens—and don't forget the longest bar.

### Swan Hill
This is also on the southern bank of the Murray, 67 km south-west of Moulamein. If we are to believe in the tales of days gone by, Swan Hill was so named because an explorer of the day, Sir Thomas Mitchell, was disturbed from his sleep early one morning by the cries of black swans in the area. The site on which he camped is now known as the Swan Hill's

Pioneer Settlement, and is one of the finest and most popular re-creations of the settlement days to be found in Australia. Nearby is the ancient paddle-steamer *Gem*, which houses various works of art and also doubles as a restaurant. Swan Hill is full of museums, including one that contains a fine collection of arms, old uniforms, and whatever else one may expect to find in a military museum. Like many other riverside townships, it has a paddle-steamer which operates from here, the *Pyap*, offering Murray cruises.

## Wodonga and Yarrawonga
Wodonga and Yarrawonga are two popular venues on the Murray, from where many good fish of all kinds are taken. The river at Yarrawonga is adjacent to Mulwala Lake, and upstream near Albury is Wodonga. Redfin are common in the main river here, along with European carp. Murray cod are also to be had, but they are normally on the small side. Golden perch appear to be virtually extinct these days above Yarrawonga, but downstream they're still to be had on baits, and sometimes on spinners, going to about 2 kg.

## MURRAY RIVER TOWNSHIPS—NEW SOUTH WALES

### Albury
Albury is the largest of the many towns that have grown up alongside the Murray in this district, and is ideally situated for fishing both on the river and in the Hume Reservoir just 12 km away. Lake Mulwala isn't so far away either, adding to the fishing potential of those stationed at Albury. The town has lots to offer the tourist or the angler killing time until the fish begin to feed in the evening. There's the Botanic Gardens at Wodonga Place, just a short walk from the main part of the town. The Ettamogah Wildlife Sanctuary is farther away—11 km north of Albury along the Hume Highway. A minimal charge is made to inspect the sanctuary, which has, apart from the usual wildlife, trees and flowers, Aboriginal artifacts and various mineral samples on display. It opens from 9 a.m. to 6 p.m. seven days a week. On the eastern bank of the Murray, facing the junction of Hume Street and Wodonga Place is the Hovell Tree Reserve, containing the gum tree marked by William Hovell, the explorer, on 17 November 1824, when he and Hamilton Hume discovered the Murray River. (I wonder what the fishing was like then?) There are many other interesting places to visit, and accommodation of most kinds is readily available.

### Balranald
A remote little town, Balranald is soon left behind for the scrubland, which hides much wildlife—emus and kangaroos, plus a heap of rabbits and God knows what else; even Bigfoot wouldn't surprise me! There's some fishing in the river here that just might produce a cod. Seven kilometres south-east of Balranald via the Sturt Highway is Yanga Lake, which is geared to all manner of water sports, including some decent fishing, but fishing exactly for what is difficult to define. We assume that the quarry will be Murray fish.

### Barham
Good redfin can be taken here in the Murray River, where they grow to quite a size. Most people come to inspect the old bridge across the river,

which connects Barham with the Victorian township of Koondrook. The bridge, built during the days of the old paddle steamers, was designed to lift up to allow the boats through, and is still in working order. But forget about the bridge and concentrate on the fishing. You shouldn't be disappointed!

## Corowa
Corowa has the Bangerang Railway (strange name that!) which runs on tracks in Ball Park, off Bridge Road and right by the Murray River, and for a small charge, the kids can ride the train while you're fishing! The 550 metres of 12-gauge track is serviced by a turntable, a locomotive shed, a station, plus two carriages pulled by a coal-fired steam engine of the 4-6-2 Pacific Steamer Class, whatever that may mean to the layman.

## Deniliquin
If Aboriginal relics are of interest then here's the place to see them, perhaps at midday, when there will be little doing on the river. The Denilakoon Exhibition has a considerable display, and is found in the Estate Building in Cressy Street. A well-presented mock-up of the town's pioneering days is also to be seen. But perhaps the most interesting feature of all is the shell collection, reputed to be one of the finest in the country. There is also a sanctuary, just off Cressy Street via a footbridge facing the Town Hall. Free-ranging kangaroos, emus and other forms of wildlife are always to be seen and can be approached quite freely. The Island Sanctuary isn't far from the centre of the town. Nearby is McLeans Beach, on the Edward River down from Charlotte Street. Clean sand and water encourage the swimmers here, and the local caravan park is close by. The Edward River is also popular for fishing. Stevens Weir on this river is located 26 km north-west of Deniliquin along the Wakool and Stevens Weir roads, where beautiful lawns down to the water's edge are ideal for a picnic.

## Jerilderie
This town's one claim to fame appears to be the fact that in February 1879 the infamous Ned Kelly and his associates raided the town, locked up the local police officers, cut the telegraph wires and then robbed the bank. The telegraph office is still there.

## Morgan Country
So called because the area used to be frequented by Mad Dan Morgan, another somewhat comical figure who later won fame as a bushranger, Morgan country offers several places of interest. The 'Mad' Dan Morgan Art Cellar situated below the Billabong Craft Centre in Railway Parade, Culcairn, contains original paintings by local and other artists, some depicting the escapades of the outlaw, and a life-sized effigy of Dan Morgan is a main attraction. The Billabong Craft Centre has first-rate hand-made articles for sale, and is also the official tourist information centre for the area. Morgans Lookout, one of the bandit's hideouts, lies 4 km north of Walla Walla, by the Alma Park Road. A wildlife refuge park isn't so far away from the lookout, and the scenery here attracts painters and photographers.

**Tocumwal**

Apart from the fishing, there's also an old aerodrome here, adjacent to the town. During the Second World War this was the site of the largest Royal Australian Air Force base in the land, but it is now used regularly by glider pilots. On the northern bank of the Murray River there's a well-developed picnic area with lawns down to the water. Vintage Second World War guns are on display, and swimming, boating and fishing are part of the scene. The fishing *must* be excellent, because the world's biggest cod is here— made of fibreglass.

# NEW ENGLAND DISTRICT

An area of striking contrasts, the New England District of New South Wales is the third largest tourist region in the state. Extending north to the Queensland border and west to the Barwon and Gwydir rivers, the southern boundary of the district stretches along the foothills of the Liverpool Range and in the east reaches the Great Dividing Range.

The New England Tableland, rising from the Moonbi Range near Tamworth, stretches 320 kilometres north to the Queensland border, and most of this mountain range is more than 900 metres above sea level. The Wollomombi Falls in the area have a drop of 500 metres, and are claimed to be the highest in the land.

Lake Keepit and Copeton Dam are probably the main fishing venues. Both are used for all kinds of water sports, and are themselves local tourist attractions. The trout streams of the New England Tableland provide some excellent trout fishing, while from the rivers of the plains come catfish, cod and yellow-belly.

Two major highways traverse the area from north to south, and good minor roads connect with most regions that have a call for them. Hidden treasure in the form of gemstones are another plus for the region, and fossickers hunt for industrial diamonds, topaz, emeralds, amethysts and other stones.

Like most other districts of New South Wales, the New England region is serviced by aircraft and trains, and by coaches from Brisbane and Melbourne, offering other choices to those who don't enjoy a long, tiresome drive. Accommodation of most types is available.

## LAKES AND STREAMS

### Lake George

Lake George is something of a mystery. Since its discovery by pioneer settler Joseph Wild in 1820, the lake has unaccountably dried up several times. This strange phenomenon has puzzled scientists for years, and, to date, the mystery surrounding it has not been solved. It last appeared as a lake in 1950, and has so far remained as the angler prefers to see it— unless it has suddenly disappeared again overnight, in which case an apology is in order.

Adjacent to the Federal Highway 40 km north of Queanbeyan, Lake George was, quite some years ago now, a noted redfin water. Some good fish were taken on baits and spinners of every kind. But as is the way with redfin, the fish suddenly increased in numbers but deteriorated in size. Now normally that's no great problem. We can't expect to catch big fish all the time. In this case, however, the change was quite dramatic. In place of the big 'uns the regulars were used to, came dozens of little fish—too tiny in fact to offer any sport at all.

Yet still the boats went out, returning with hundreds of dead redfin proudly stacked at the anglers' feet. It is difficult to imagine what kind of kick this brought them, but I believe that anyone who slaughters fish of any kind in that sort of quantity isn't an angler at all—he's a killer, out to get whatever moves before him.

Exactly what the situation is today with Lake George is difficult to say, but the potential was there once and may well return. Redfin are notorious for fading out like that, and then reappearing for no apparent reason. The tidal reaction of the lake makes it a dangerous water to boat on. There are a few facilities on the foreshore.

### The streams

The high altitude of the New England District accounts for the lower temperatures necessary for the acclimatisation of the cold-water species. Here the streams contain mainly trout—some in fact are renowned for their trout fishing; but so many streams exist in the area that it's difficult to know where to begin.

Most of the icy streams encourage a good rate of growth in the fish and are worth a visit when the time is ripe, usually when the banks are alive with insects which are blown on the water. A rising stream may have the same effect by washing worms, slugs, and other such creatures into the water where the fish soon become conditioned to accepting them as a natural part of their present diet.

The best New England streams include the headwaters of the Murray–Darling system, such as the MacDonald River and its tributaries in the mountainous region of Walcha. North of Glen Innes the Deepwater River is another fine fishing stream, as is the Gwydir River and tributaries like the Ollera and George, the Booralong, Sandy and Moredon creeks. Mere creeks they may be, but each supports some decent fish. The Gwydir River is found in the rugged terrain west of Guyra. Flowing westward, the river and creeks contain worthwhile rainbow trout which occasionally reach 3 kg.

Eastwards the streams make for the Pacific, after riding the eastern falls. They include the noteworthy Rockvale Creek near Armidale, which flows through grazing country before plunging over Wollomombi Falls and into the Macleay gorges. Boundary Creek, tributary to Rockvale Creek, is equally productive. Both offer splendid trout fishing for their entire length, although local knowledge about the exact areas is a great asset.

Some 80 kilometres or so east of Armidale and Rockvale runs an assortment of streams, all providing some first-rate trout fishing. Many go under such odd names as the Guy Fawkes, Jocks Water, Styx, Serpentine and Oaky. The Little Nymboida and Little Murray also offer good fishing. They're lovely little streams, skipping through timbered and grazing land as they hurry on to the gorges.

Nymph-fishing seems the practice on these streams. Brown and black nymphs are perhaps the most popular, in one variation or another, but the green nymph has its uses also. Dry flies suggested include Greenwell's glory, coachman, white and brown moths and the mayfly. Wet fly patterns are the black and red matuka, grasshopper, cockybondhu, coachman, black gnat, Greenwell's glory and the Alexandra.

24

Very light bait-fishing with a sinker-free line is also recommended. Natural bait-casting with a fly rod is probably the élite form of fishing a bait, half-way between the normal way of presenting a bait and actual fly-fishing. Tiny worms, grubs, grasshoppers and crickets, almost any natural insect, can be put on the water with care by the use of a fly rod, and once mastered, this method gives the angler a most delicate and killing way of getting amongst the fish when normal bait-fishing tactics won't move them.

Armidale is the accepted centre of some of the finest trout fishing. It is also the headquarters of the New England Trout Acclimatisation Society, which takes a lively interest in the subject of trout fishing, breeding and adaptability to this district.

## THE ORANA DISTRICT

'Orana' is the Aboriginal word for 'welcome', and the beauty of this region certainly welcomes the traveller. Perhaps nowhere else in New South Wales are there such breathtaking scenes. Rivers and lakes, mountains and streams, hills and forests, valleys and caverns—the Orana area has them all.

Wildlife in abundance roams the plains from dawn till dusk in this unspoilt territory where the rivers and streams run crystal clear and clean, nursing along in their flow the Murray species of fish—cod, golden perch, catfish, black bream; it's claimed they're queuing to entertain us in the rivers that whisper past the trees.

The district is the largest in the state, covering 200 000 square kilometres of land that is severed in places by the Bogan, Castlereagh, Macintyre, Macquarie, Gwydir, Namoi and Barwon rivers, to mention a few. Most head north or north-west to rendezvous with the Darling River.

For the field photographer there's no end to the scope he'll find here. The fossicker will be equally at home, with the region rich in mineral deposits. The black opals of Lightning Ridge are world renowned for their shimmering beauty. But the gems we seek will be in the rivers and the dams. The big Burrendong Dam lies 31 km south-east of Wellington, where the Macquarie and Cudgegong rivers meet. We'll be there too, trying for an introduction to the fine fish secure in the depths of the dam.

Despite its unspoilt appearance, the region is well served with modern accommodation, with first-class caravan parks and camping areas established at the most popular spots.

### LAKES AND DAMS

#### Burrendong Dam

Usually referred to as the main dam in the region, the Burrendong Dam is certainly geared to take visitors in its stride. To reach the dam travel 5 km south of Wellington on the Mitchell Highway, then turn left onto the Mumbil Road for 16 km. Turn left again and motor on for a further 6 km to the main wall. Drive across the wall and continue onto the spillway. At last you're there, but the journey's been worthwhile.

The Burrendong Dam checks the waters of the Cudgegong and Macquarie rivers. When full the lake covers 8903 hectares, with a maximum depth of 56 metres. The construction of the dam is unique in that, although destined to provide water for irrigation and to mitigate flooding, those concerned in the venture were able to foresee its potential for public recreation, and steps were taken at the beginning to build the dam with the public's needs in mind.

All dangerous debris was removed from the water to make it safe for the boating and water-skiing enthusiasts who make good use of the dam, although some may have been left to afford the fish some shelter from the heat of the day and also around which to congregate.

Two separate State Recreation Areas are set aside for those who wish to muck about in, on, or around the banks of the water. Burrendong State Recreation Area is found immediately south of the dam wall. The other is situated north-east of Sturt Town. There are facilities for day and overnight visitors in both areas and rangers are in residence to supervise activities. They probably know where the fish are biting. so why not ask them?

### Narran Lake
Situated approximately 96 km due west of Walgett via the Cumborah Road. Invested with the honour of being one of the largest, yet least known, of the natural inland lakes, Narran Lake provides no facilities for the visitor, who must therefore manage as best as he can if bent on investigating the potential for fishing here, about which there is little information. Arrangements can be made to fly over the area in light aircraft. The phone number to call if interested is Walgett 344. Wild animals and birdlife are a part of the scene here, and huge gatherings of pelicans converge during the mating season to settle on the tiny islands in the lake.

### THE RIVER SCENE
The headwaters of the Darling River are in Queensland. It travels south, and for most of the year is reduced to a series of waterholes. At Wentworth it enters Victoria to team up with the Murray River. Joining the Darling are some of the streams already mentioned in this section, and each supplies the angler with some worthwhile sport. The following are just a few of the interesting places related to the streams, and each offers some fishing to the visitor.

### Bourke
Just 4 km from Bourke, west along Anson Street, then right for a further kilometre, we come to a lock and a weir on the Darling River. But no ordinary weir and lock these—they were constructed in 1897 to ensure a water supply for Bourke, while at the same time allowing for the passage of the many large steamers that travelled up and down the river in those days. Six km north of Bourke along the Mitchell Highway is a lift-up bridge. With a centre span that was raised to let the steamers through, the bridge was opened to traffic in 1883, and today is a well known feature of the area. A legend connected with the bridge insists that once a person has crossed the bridge he will surely return to Bourke—but that would depend on the fishing, wouldn't it?

### Brewarrina
Now here's an interesting site to visit—an old Aboriginal fishery. Located just off the northern end of Sandon Street, in the bed of the Darling River just downstream of the weir, there are some stone-walled fish traps. Some

are still standing, even if not in one piece, and are just some of the odd Aboriginal relics that are to be found in the Brewarrina area. The traps were used to catch all kinds of fish in the Darling.

**Norfolk and Bald Hill Creek Falls**
A brace of waterfalls not to be missed, set as they are in breathtaking scenery. The heavily timbered Warung State Forest acts as a natural stage within which the cascading crystal-clear and sparkling streams plunge to the depths below. The Norfolk Falls hit the pool at the bottom after a sheer drop of 43 metres. The rainbow trout in the pool add their very own splash of colour as they leap from the water to greet the rejuvenating falls. The Bald Hill Creek Falls is unique in its geological character, resembling in structure the Giants Causeway in County Antrim, Northern Ireland. The 567-hectare Norfolk Flora Reserve offers beautiful scenery and its deep creek gorges are frequented by wombats, kangaroos and other creatures, while the tree tops host an assortment of birds, including at times the rare black cockatoo. To find the falls, go 2 km east of Coolah along the Cassilis Road, turn left onto the Coolah Creek Road, then turn right after 23 km and travel a further 13 km to the signpost in the Warung State Forest. Caravans are unable to use this road. A picnic area with barbecue facilities and freshwater is found at the end of the road near the Norfolk Falls. Don't forget the camera.

**Mudgee**
Travel 3 km north-east of Mudgee on the Gulgong Road, turn left on Hargraves Road for 11 km, and then right on to the road that leads to the Cudgegong River Park. Situated on the eastern foreshores of the huge Burrendong Dam, the park is ideal for water sports. It's a bit crowded in summer, but don't let that stop you. Get the rods out and elbow your way in, because there's some really fine fishing to be had here, with Murray cod, catfish, golden perch or yellow-belly and even the occasional trout. First-rate camping facilities are found within the park, and details concerning them may be obtained from the park ranger.

**Trangie**
Here we have the Gin Gin Weir. To reach it drive north-east from Trangie along the Collie Road for 16 km, turn right on the Warren–Narromine Road before crossing the bridge for another 6 km. Then finally turn left at the signpost to follow the track 3 km to the weir. And let's hope it was worth it! The weir was built in 1896, but due to flood damage had to be rebuilt in 1902. More floods leaving more damage behind them have resulted in a somewhat jaded weir—but that doesn't affect the fishing! There is boating above the pool, and fishing there will bring good catches of Murray cod and yellow-belly.

**Warren**
The Macquarie Marshes are in fact a huge depression in the ground filled by the waters of the Macquarie River. Surrounded by peculiar plants that were evolved by the very nature of their unusual habitat to withstand the effects of being left high and dry and then inundated with water almost simultaneously, the marshes are a haven for birdlife. I suspect that at times a few fish must get in there too, but it's the birds that draw the

crowds. Ducks, swans, pelicans, cormorants, ibis, spoonbills—they're all to be seen in the marshes. When conditions are right, flat-bottomed punts take visitors via a series of weed-choked channels to the centre of the marshes. Such an expedition covers many kilometres through the kind of terrain rarely witnessed on this earth, and the wildlife adds even more to the scene. To get there travel 93 km north of Warren on the Carinda–Warren Road, turn right into the Willie–Quambone Road. Carry on for about 8 km from the turn-off—this road cuts through to the marshes. Visitors then proceed on to Quambone and then back to Warren. For conducted tours contact the Warren Tourist Information Centre in Burton Street.

## THE RIVERINA

Through this region of New South Wales wanders one of Australia's longest rivers— the 1690-kilometre-long Murrumbidgee; wide, deep, and with precious little flow as it creeps along to meet the Murray near Balranald. The Murrumbidgee (Aboriginal for 'big water') rises 30 km north of Kiandra in the Snowy Mountains and on its long journey travels through the Riverina from east to west. By the end of its run it will have absorbed the waters of many other streams—the Molonglo, Yass, Cotter and Goodradigbee in the Australian Capital Territory, to the Tumut River near Gundagai. Although it gains these waters, the Murrumbidgee also parts with some to feed the Burrinjuck Dam and the series of channels that create the Murrumbidgee Irrigation Areas. It is also joined by the Lachlan River from the west of this district.

There are golden perch, some Murray cod and similar species at times in most reaches of the Murrumbidgee, with trout available in the higher sections where it is more suitable to them. Fishing techniques vary little from those used on the Murray, but wherever possible it is advisable to use locally obtained baits.

The country is pleasant, and easily travelled by major highways and roads linking the main centres. There are good caravan and camping facilities by lakeside or river, where the angler can fish to his heart's content. In the east are heavily timbered mountain slopes and valleys. The main centre of the Riverina is Wagga Wagga—always worth a visit—and, being almost on the banks of the Murrumbidgee, is perhaps a good place for a base.

### Gundagai

In addition to the Dog on the Tucker Box waiting patiently to be fed, there are other attractions at Gundagai. There's some fishing to be had close by in the Murrumbidgee and Tumut rivers, and organised canoe trips begin from here, lasting for no less than six days. These expeditions are not unduly expensive because all equipment, meals, tuition and accommodation are included. These tours operate during the summer months, and include canoeing up both rivers. Those interested should contact Canoe Tours Australia, c/o The Old Hospital, Otway Street, Gundagai, NSW 2722.

### Hay District

Fifty-eight kilometres west of Hay on the Murrumbidgee River is Maude Weir, offering some excellent fishing from beautiful lawns that also have facilities for picnics and barbecues. But if that doesn't satisfy the kids then take them along to Hay Gaol Museum. (It might be an idea to leave them there!) The museum is in Church Street, a brisk walk north-east of the Post Office and past the Olympic pool. Relics from the old pioneer days are the attraction here, with a century-old Cobb & Co coach that is still used for festive occasions. It appeared in the film *Mad Dog Morgan*.

## Murrumbidgee Irrigation Areas
Within this region we have the Inland Fisheries Research Station 6 km south-east of Narrandera, just off the Sturt Highway. Here, important research is focused on the species of fish of the inland waterways. There is also a fish reference collection and a laboratory for research. During October, November and December, a fully comprehensive breeding programme gets under way, and between January and April, tiny native fish may be purchased for the fish-tank. Set in delightful grounds are the station's growing ponds. Nearby is the Lake Talbot Swimming Pool Complex—just 2 km south-east of the Narrandera Post Office. Here a $250 000 complex awaits the visitor who wants a dip in the Olympic swimming pool. There are pools for toddlers too, set in a bushland sanctuary with picnic facilities available.

It's the adjoining Lake Talbot, however, that holds the most promise, for here we can water-ski, swim, canoe, sail, and, oh yes, fish. We then have Berembed Weir, a bit further away from Narrandera, 40 km south-east of the town. The weir helps to supply water to the area and was originally built in 1910. Its sole purpose is to channel water from the Murrumbidgee River into the main canal that functions as the area's irrigation lifeline. Picnics, barbecues, and even camping is permitted here, but there are no toilets or other amenities. Another weir is found 22 km south-west of Leeton, where extensive lawns and coin-operated gas barbecues make it well worth a visit. Gogeldrie Weir is also part of the irrigation scheme accepting and distributing water to help the process along. Fishing, water-skiing and boating can be done nearby. And if the fish aren't biting we then move on to Griffith, heading out 8 km north-west of the town to call in at Lake Wyangan, a beautiful sheet of water that is used extensively at weekends by sailing, water-skiing, rowing, swimming, motor-boating and fishing enthusiasts. All the facilities are here, from picnic grounds to children's paddling pools, but unfortunately there are no amenities for campers. There are many other places of interest in the Murrumbidgee Irrigation Areas, including zoos and museums, and for a family holiday the district has a lot to offer.

## Wagga Wagga
Here are found research centres, institutes, and colleges of advanced education that interest us not in the least. There is, however, a lake in Wagga Wagga worth mentioning, and that's Albert Lake, just 6 km south of the township and geared to all the usual water sports, including fishing. Alongside the lake is the golf club, and the boating club, where visitors are welcome. The Murray Cod Hatcheries and Fauna Park are worth a visit. Situated 8 km east of Wagga Wagga, all the Murray species of fish are bred for sale to farmers wishing to stock their ponds; fish acclimatisation societies; fishing clubs; government bodies—they're all in the fish-buying game. Contained within the hatchery is the largest Murray cod in captivity.

This and other native fish swim in large aquariums, but it's the giant cod that draws the crowds—it weighs 52 kg and is 1.4 metres long. Imagine that on the end of a line if you dare! There are also many animals and birds in the Fauna Park, and children are encouraged to feed a midget bull, donkeys, a camel, and Shetland ponies, as well as other animals.

## THE SNOWY MOUNTAINS DISTRICT

The Snowy Mountains region of New South Wales is one of extreme climatic changes. The valleys and a few of the picturesque lakes are a direct result of the imperceptible movement of glaciers and the towering cloud-tipped peaks the work of erosion over millions of years, so that we are left with many scenes pretty enough for a picture card.

So contrasting is the weather, however, that the delightful warmth of a soft spring day may change within the hour to a blinding blizzard. Mist and drizzle on the lower plains may be replaced by the rays of a dazzling sun as the traveller treks towards the higher plateaus.

In winter the temperatures remain around freezing point, and there is snow on the ground for months. Travel at such times becomes hazardous, and the use of snow chains on vehicles headed for the skiing and fishing re' orts is a sure sign that the drivers have been this way before.

It is the fishing alone that interests us here, and in this magnificent mountain retreat the lakes, the rivers and the streams present us with just the kind of fishing we'd expect to find in this high-rise wonderland. Highly spirited rainbows and browns, so reminiscent of the spray-flecked mountain streams, abound in all the waters in the Snowy.

There's the Snowy River itself, once celebrated as tip-top trout territory, before man took a hand in damming it to form the Jindabyne; and the Murrumbidgee, with the excellent sport it provides for most of its length. The Thredbo, Geehi, and Eucumbene rivers are just a few more. And then there are the lakes—the illustrious Eucumbene, mighty and proud of the vast area it dominates up there in the hills, and the Jindabyne, inferior in size but not in potential as it challenges the Eucumbene itself to equal the magnificent trout the Jindabyne is producing these days.

We then have the lesser dams—Tantangara, Talbingo, Khancoban, and last but by no means least the moody but equally mighty Blowering Dam, second largest of them all, in the Snowy Mountains Hydro-electric Authority (what a terrible name for such a beautiful area!).

I have omitted other waters, not because they don't warrant a place here but simply because space won't allow them, but every one is there for the angler's enjoyment. Yes, there are huge trout in them there hills, and plenty of them! Convoys of vehicles with their boats in tow head for the mountains and the lakes, the rivers and the streams from all over the country, and it's no secret that once anglers have sampled the fishing to be had, they'll return again and again for more. That's the trouble with the Snowy, once you've been bitten by the bug there's no cure . . .

### LAKES AND DAMS

#### Blowering Dam

Second largest of all the dams in the Snowy province, the Blowering Dam is controlled by the Department of Conservation and used for irrigation. The fluctuation of the water level here creates a set of conditions that is hardly conducive to good fishing. Some fairly big trout (great, compared to standards in other states) of up to 4 kg have been netted in the past, although the ever-increasing shoals of redfin in the water leave some doubt about the future potential of the Blowering Dam as a true trout water. There are very few suitable spawning streams to help the trout propagate the species so the angler must expect a smaller bag than those normally taken elsewhere. Apart from this dampening survey, it's also necessary to add that there are no official camping and caravan sites, so the visitor will have to find his own.

## Lake Eucumbene

Lake Eucumbene is by far the most noted trout water in the land. It was created in 1957, and the magnificent brown and rainbow trout taken from its depths have helped considerably in making the names of some of the most prominent angling writers around, writers who have passed on their experiences of tangling with the fish through the medium of the angling press.

Credited with being seven times the size of Sydney Harbour, Lake Eucumbene is the largest of all the lakes, reservoirs and dams in Australia. As it was formed originally as a water catchment for the area, I assume that the fishing it offers is quite incidental; but how well it lends itself to the sport, encouraging anglers in their droves back to its banks each year.

Some great trout have been, and still are being, lured from this phenomenal water on spoons, plugs, flies and baits of many kinds, and each has its disciples who swear their choice is the best. To be as dogmatic as that is to invite failure because here, as much as anywhere else, changing conditions must dictate to us the most likely temptation to bring about results. Experience of a water can help tremendously, yet even the most knowledgeable of the dry fly experts must fail at times, when the fish are more interested in a morsel on the bottom or at mid-water than anything floating on the top, so it pays to be fairly proficient with every technique, whether it be roaming the banks with a spinner, static with a bait, or dropping a fly softly on the water.

Mainly because most anglers pursue them in such a fashion, the majority of trout are probably taken by trolling or spinning from a boat or the bank, and the lures used appear to be very much a personal choice. The newcomer can merely study what others use, through the lens of a pair of binoculars if necessary; and don't be put off by a few rude gestures—acknowledge them in a similar friendly manner.

During November to April, the fly-fishing fanatics move in, and you can bet your bottom dollar that among them will be some of the finest wand-wielders in the country, fishing with fly sticks longer than those normally encountered on the crystal-clear mountain streams. They appreciate fully the extra distance a rod of three metres can gain them when coupled with a suitable line. And in their fly boxes will be found among other patterns tiny black and brown nymphs, black and brown ants, the Alexandra, muddler minnow, Dixon's mudeye, the Mrs Simpson, black matuka, cockybondhu, black phantom and the fuzzy wuzzy. Most will focus their fishing on the magical moments of sunset and dawn.

Those who prefer to bait-fish (and there are a good many who do) will find the months of winter and spring the best in which to make their bid

Some tend to fish their bait on the bottom with a running sinker attached to the line, while others depend more heavily on a bubble float with the bait fished at a profitable depth below it, but exactly what that depth might be depends largely on the location fished and the conditions at the waterside. Experimenting at different depths is one way to solve the problem; another is to keep an eye on those who look as if they've got it together. Be sure though that while you're shooting furtive glances at them, they're not doing likewise, or you'll all be in the soup.

The most commonly used baits are scrubworms and mudeyes, the latter being obtainable from sunken branches close into the edge. However, after travelling the long distances that most anglers do who fish here, it would be a pity if no mudeyes were found, so don't take such a risk—take an ample supply of bait along with you. If you don't, that trip of a lifetime may well be spent hunting high and low for baits that simply aren't available at that time.

As in the case of Victoria's huge Eildon Reservoir, the Eucumbene consists of a number of 'bays', and the fishing will vary with the level of the water. Each is open to the angler throughout the year, though it is hoped that few anglers appear during a period when the trout are obviously breeding.

**Adaminaby** (map ref. 1) boasts of the largest trout in the world. It's a real whopper—16 metres long, and a sight to gladden the heart of any sportsman. True, it's made of fibreglass, but looks most real and effective—the colouring is superb. Obviously, we can't expect to catch them quite that big here, but the area of Adaminaby (and Old Adaminaby, set right on the lake) is well geared to cater for the angler's needs—camping and caravan sites, motel and hotel, cabins and even a sporting store. Launching ramps and boat hire are available at Paddy's Boats. Cottages, units, and a caravan park are also available at Old Adaminaby. Some good trolling is to be had here, and average bait fishing. There are plenty of trees and rocky outcrops, but the area tends to be windy at times.

**Anglers Reach** (map ref. 2) offers some very fine fishing. Located where the old Adaminaby–Kiandra Road disappears into the lake, it is approximately 8 km from Old Adaminaby on the northern side of the lake. Anglers Reach is one of the largest resorts on the lake, and is well able to meet the visitor's demands for accommodation and boat hire. There is a small village here, with stores that stock fishing gear.

**Braemar** (map ref. 3) is situated 4 km from the Eucumbene Dam wall, and has the usual camping/caravan/boat-hire facilities so prominent at each popular area of the lake. The shores are heavily timbered, and offer good bait-fishing to the one who isn't afraid to lose a hook or two—or perhaps several dozen by the time he heads off home again, but remember that wherever snags are to be found so are fish. Some excellent trolling is also there for those who can keep off the snags on the bottom and, if the fly-fisher concentrates on the south-west corner of the bay, he should also get into the action.

**Buckenderra** (map ref. 4) has a large camping complex covering 25 hectares, consisting of self-contained villas, on-site caravans and seven-metre four-berth cruisers. There is a fleet of runabouts available for hire, and many camping and caravan parks are established near the lake.

Other facilities include a children's playground, store and service station. Buckenderra is claimed to be the most developed resort on the lake and from here the angler can reach such celebrated fishing spots as the Rushy Plain Bay, Middlingbank, and the Frying Pan Arm. First-rate fishing of all kinds is found at Buckenderra and the waters nearby.

*Frying Pan* (map ref. 5)—and with a name like that there's simply got to be a feed here for the angler! Some exciting fly-fishing may be had here, especially in O'Neills Bay, and on the upper parts of the arm. Trolling, spinning and bait-fishing are also exceptionally good. There is plenty of rocky terrain around the shores, and launching ramps and boat-hire are available. Close to the lake are a camp-site and caravan park, fishing lodge and sporting stores.

Those are just a few of the more popular parts of Lake Eucumbene, and each is able to deal fully with the visiting angler's needs. To avoid disappointment after a trip of perhaps many hundreds of kilometres I suggest that accommodation and boat-hire be confirmed beforehand, and that the newcomer to the lake studies all available literature to lessen the chances of a fishless visit. Seek local advice where possible, and act upon it until you are able to establish for yourself what fishing this wide expanse of water is all about.

Those intending to fish from a powered runabout should take note of the hazards of strong winds mentioned extensively in all that has been written about the Eucumbene. The high altitude in which the water is set accounts for winds that can create a few problems for the uninitiated, so study this point carefully—it's not included here just for interest, but as a warning that should be heeded before ever setting out on the water. A few fish missed because the water's too rough to ride out is one thing, but a member of a party missing is quite another altogether.

Boat-hire is available at the following:
*Braemar Caravan Park;* launching, 5 km past Eucumbene Dam.
*Anglers Reach;* R. M. and R. C. Berry; petrol, launching.
*Old Adaminaby;* Paddy's Boats.
*Frying Pan Creek;* Mr J. Valentine.
*Buckenderra* (Middlingbank); Buckenderra Holiday Centre.


## Lake Jindabyne

Although a first-rate water in its own right, Lake Jindabyne, and every other water near enough to be affected, is unfortunately overshadowed by the Big Brother image of the Eucumbene. This is a pity because many anglers believe the Jindabyne to be the better of the two. Certainly the trout fishing is on a par with that of the larger dam and very often leaves it for dead, so that placed anywhere else the Jindabyne would stand alone as the water supreme.

The Eucumbene is larger, of course, occupying an area equal to seven times that of the Jindabyne, which is nevertheless still the size of Sydney Harbour (I wonder why the Harbour is always used as a comparison?), and that's a hell of a lot of water to troll.

In more recent years a bonus in the shape of Atlantic salmon has added spice to the angling here. These were released into the lake by officials of the Gaden Trout Hatchery who, like their associates in other states, are doing a good job of maintaining the unique fishing available to us, though they receive very little recognition for their effort.

Plump, spangled brook trout are also in the Jindabyne, yet they rarely appear. However, it is mainly the lure of the big brown and rainbow trout that captures the imagination, and these are the species of fish that most anglers hope to intercept. Angling techniques appear to differ little from those used on the Eucumbene, so when you first arrive ask the advice of locals with experience of fishing the two waters in all conditions. This is the fastest and surest way of finding out what's being caught and where— and on which fly, bait, or lure.

Most areas around the shoreline of the lake are worth more than just a cursory glance, two of the more popular being Hatchery Bay, situated on the western side of the water, and Waste Point, at the northern tip. Here, the deeper water provides many fine fish to those who have taken the trouble to learn all that they possibly could about the region before wetting a line. It goes without saying that a well-detailed map of the entire Snowy Mountains area will be invaluable to those contemplating a visit.

### Khancoban Pondage
This is a beautiful sheet of water set in delightful surroundings. Some exceptionally big trout have been taken from the pondage, which is situated near the township of Khancoban. Launching sites are to be found by turning right to the water between Murray Switching Station and Murray 2 Power Station. Fishing licences and gear, boat-hire and advice can be obtained at the Shell Service Station. There is accommodation at the caravan park in Alpine Way (pets allowed), or at the licensed Alpine Inn, Alpine Way (check for pets).

### Talbingo Dam
A long, narrow stretch of water with a reputation for good trout fishing and based in the Tumut River Gorge, this dam is not the most accessible of waters, but well worth the effort to give it a go. Rough and rugged, it has the added attraction of beautiful surroundings. The Talbingo Dam wall is the highest of any dam wall in the Snowy Mountains—158.5 metres. Reputed to be well stocked with trout, this water is nevertheless not heavily fished, so here's one place that surely warrants a visit or two. Talbingo Dam was the last to be filled, and like most others has the usual amenities. Boats may be rented in the area and launched close to the dam wall above the town of Talbingo.

### Tantangara Dam
This water is situated at the headwaters of the Murrumbidgee River and actually flows through a tunnel into Lake Eucumbene at Providence Portal. Well stocked with rainbows and particularly browns, Tantangara Dam is fishing very well, according to current reports. This water lends itself readily to the fly-fisher's gear when there are suitable conditions at the water's edge. The dam lies 35 km from Adaminaby, a town well able to serve as a base for the many waters within reasonable distance of it. For those who prefer to sleep under canvas there's a camping ground for their use.

## TROUT STREAMS

In addition to the array of dams in the Snowy Mountains region, there are numerous rivers and streams, most of which are closed to anglers from the beginning of May to November. This period may vary in different waters, so the would-be visitor should either check this matter out first or risk falling foul of the law. There are also a few 'fly only' waters, one being the Moonbah River, acclaimed by some as the finest fly-water in the land, with a reputation for supporting some extra-large trout. The following are just a few selected rivers and streams of the many awaiting the skilled fly-fisherman.

### Eucumbene River

Consistently good fishing is to be found near the dam, where quiet pools surrounded by reasonably clear banks offer some pleasant fishing. Browns and rainbows collect here in great numbers when conditions are right, and that's when the rainbows and then the browns head for their spawning grounds during the first months of winter. They then gather in shoals along the river, an amazing spectacle for those lucky enough to be there at the time. It's said they can often be seen in their thousands, and many are brought to the angler's net. Farther up from the dam some excellent fishing can be had 25 km from Adaminaby, where there are also some interesting creeks to be tried.

### Geehi River

There is a cluster of tiny trout streams in the area of the Geehi River and village. The Geehi is a grand dry-fly water in its own right, and one not to be passed over lightly. Some 80 km from Jindabyne, it nests in a most delightful setting. The streams located nearby are the Wilkinsons, Bridge, and the Bogong. The Geehi Dam and Windy Creek Pondage can be reached from here by a track alongside the main river. A better road leads to the dam at Khancoban, 27 km away.

### Moonbah River

The Moonbah River, occasionally known as the Mowamba is a 'fly only' water, considered to be the most productive of its kind in Australia, and therefore it beckons to the top fly-fishers each year. Not a water to be easily mastered, it is nevertheless worth the time and effort to try to do just that, because some very big fish are prepared to meet those capable of outsmarting them. Situated approximately 10 km below Jindabyne, this water is well worth a visit by those planning to concentrate mainly on the lake. It will offer a nice change of pace at least . . .

### Murrumbidgee River

One of the better known rivers in the region, the Murrumbidgee is almost as popular as the big lakes. It is not a particularly big fish water, but nevertheless carries enough trout for most of its length to satisfy the army of anglers who fish it regularly. Just 6 km from Adaminaby, the Murrumbidgee begins its journey at the headwaters near the Tantangara Dam, and continues right down to the southern plains. It is from Adaminaby that you can reach Bolaro in no time at all, and this part of the Murrumbidgee is especially worthy of some added attention. Several fly-fishing streams converge with the headwaters of the Murrumbidgee to add further to its attraction. These are the Boggy Plains, Tantangara, and Nungar creeks, the last being by far the most favoured.

## Snowy River

No list, however limited, of the Snowy Mountains rivers and streams can be compiled without mention of the Snowy River, if only because of its name. Its entry here, however, is on merit alone, which is well deserved. Its potential has lessened considerably since the creation of Lake Jindabyne, which called for the damming of the Snowy, yet since the lake itself has turned up fishing trumps, it may be argued that the decline in sport on the Snowy River is made up by that to be had from the dam. The river is reached downstream from Jindabyne by the road from Berridale to Dalgety. You get to the upstream reaches from Jindabyne by following the road to Mount Kosciusko.

Other rivers worth mentioning here are the Thredbo, Yarrangobilly, Tumut, Murray, Delegate, Maclaughlin . . . The list is long, and each river has that special quality to classify it as a trout stream. Indeed, in any other place they would be renowned for the unique fishing they give us, yet up there in the Snowy Mountains they're simply run-of-the-mill!

## BAITS, LURES AND FLIES

Although most regular visitors to the Snowy Mountains will defend vigorously the attributes of certain baits, lures and flies, the fact remains that a wide variety of each is used with varying degrees of success, and that often the misguided loyalty an angler has for whatever adorns the end of his line is apt to put him at a disadvantage. The offering that catches fish at any particular time or place is the one to use on that occasion, and unless the angler concerned has no prior experience of fishing a water, he can only discover what that might be by trial and error, or possibly from local fishermen prepared to give him a helping hand. So the following are only suggestions, given to me by anglers who have over the years fished the Snowy Mountains waters with considerable success, though they would not be too proud to try something entirely unorthodox if they suddenly found themselves fishless.

*Baits* Generally these consist of either a mudeye or a large milky scrubworm. The latter can occasionally be gathered from the flats well enough away from the water's edge to be left high and dry. Mudeyes can be found clinging to timbers in the water from September through to December, when bait-fishing tends to deteriorate. It is perhaps an act of folly, nevertheless, to rely completely on the chance encounter of baits in this manner, and the wise angler will obtain at least a small supply of baits beforehand. A new trend is beginning to emerge at Lake Eucumbene—the use of yabbies for bait. The bed of the dam is now believed to be littered with them, and the fish are conditioned to accept them as a major part of their diet. A yabbie is fixed to a hook small enough to accept it snugly, then cast out and allowed to sink in the wake of a single split-shot. When on the bottom the bait is recovered slowly but enticingly by a flick of the rod top. This technique is said to have claimed some very good brownies lately.

*Lures* The number of different lures being used in the dams and some of the rivers is simply too great to be listed here in full; however, the following will give some idea of those credited with some success. The celta, in either red and black, green and black, red and gold or silver and green is said to capture more trout than any other spinner. The flatfish, wonder wobbler, super duper, Baltic minnow, Eucumbene spoon, Shakespeare reflex, and the Devon can also be relied upon, but when one fails another should be tried without delay. Attention should also be focused on their colour, because certain conditions cause some colours to get better response than others, so give each a try until one is stopped in its tracks by a mighty fish.

*Wet Flies* Some suggested wet flies are the black fuzzy wuzzy, muddler minnow, in either black, black and white or grey, Alexandra, yellow hopper, and the black and red matuka. A few useful nymphs will include the hare's ear, March brown, black gnat and the stone fly.

*Dry Flies* The favoured flies here are the coachman, red and black spinner, Greenwell's glory, cockybondhu, butcher, hair-wing, royal coachman, and others which appear to be similar. Weight-forward tapers and shooting-heads are very much a part of the scene on the big dams, for these lines in the right hands increase distance tremendously. An extra-long rod will also aid casting.

## PLACES OF INTEREST
Away up in the Snowy Mountains are many interesting places that deserve a visit while the fish aren't biting. Some are mentioned below for the touring angler's attention.

### Gaden Trout Hatchery
Each trout chaser should feel obliged to call in at the hatchery simply to see what goes on there. Research into the hatching and rearing of Atlantic salmon, brook trout and rainbows is more involved than most would appreciate. Approximately half a million baby trout are bred at the hatchery each year, and most are released in the nearby streams. Atlantic salmon and brook trout raised there now swim in the Jindabyne. To help the projects along a small fee is charged for entry to the hatchery, where barbecue facilities are available, plus the opportunity of a hot shower nearby. The Gaden Trout Hatchery is on the banks of the Thredbo River 6 km west of Jindabyne.

### Grace Lea Island Animal Sanctuary
This is always good for a visit even when the fish are biting, because the sanctuary is on an island actually within Lake Eucumbene—the angler can thus look for possible spots to fish while travelling on the launch that operates from Old Adaminaby. So delighted are the animals to see us there that they come down to the water's edge to enjoy their tucker.

### Kosciusko National Park
An Information Centre here gives the visiting angler the latest, up-to-the-minute news about which water is fishing the best. But quite apart from that, the park is worth a visit simply to see the wonderful birdlife, and perhaps some of the animals that live and breed freely in their natural

surroundings. The centre is open 8.30 a.m. to 4.30 p.m. daily. It's a beautiful spot, and if you wish to linger a caravan park and cabins will meet everyone's needs. Situated at Sawpit Creek on the Mount Kosciusko Road, the park lies 20 km west of Jindabyne. A bus service in winter runs to Smiggin Holes and Perisher Valley.

## Southern Cloud Park
Located on the Snowy Mountains Highway just west of Cooma is a memorial to the *Southern Cloud*. Believed to have gone down in the sea in 1931, the plane was virtually stumbled upon in 1958 by a workman from the Snowy Mountains Hydro-electric Authority in the Deep Creek area. With the memorial is some wreckage of the aircraft and a recorded tape recounts the story of the *Southern Cloud*. Since Cooma is known as the gateway to the Snowy, and most travellers pass through there, a slight detour to the memorial would be well justified.

## Yarrangobilly Caves
Also on the Snowy Mountains Highway, 113 km north of Cooma, these caves are in the northern part of the Kosciusko National Park, within the huge limestone deposit in the valley of the Yarrangobilly River, a tributary of the Murrumbidgee and Tumut rivers. Open to visitors at 11 a.m., 1 p.m., and 3 p.m. daily, the caves were discovered in 1834. Although about 60 caves are known to exist in the area, only four have so far been made available to the public. Each has well constructed paths with safety railings and are well illuminated to highlight their calcite formations. A thermal pool amidst delightful surroundings is also worth a look. Picnic tables and fireplaces are available for the public's use, as is a toilet block, but there is no food or accommodation to be had. An entrance fee to the Yarrangobilly Caves is charged, and tickets must be obtained first from the Visitors Centre, open 8.30 a.m. to 4.30 p.m. daily.

## Additional Information
In November each year there is a trout festival at Adaminaby, and the major prize is usually worth more than a thousand dollars. The festival runs for a week, and in addition to the major prize many others are to be won. Visitors and residents may enter the contest free of charge, and weighing-in stations will be situated at most of the more popular venues. Some good fish can be expected because, in the past, brown trout of more than 10 kg are said to have been taken, although the New South Wales record is officially held by a fish of 9 kg taken on a wonder wobbler near Providence Portal, Lake Eucumbene, in 1969.

# SOUTH-EASTERN DISTRICT
Apart from the Snowy Mountains region of New South Wales, the south-eastern part of this state embraces many rivers and lakes outside the sphere of the Snowy, most of which have a great deal to offer the angler in search of some sport. The south-eastern area, for our purposes, also includes the fishing of the Australian Capital Territory.

The Burrinjuck Dam, for example, is known almost as widely as the Eucumbene, as are the trout it supports. The Murray and Murrumbidgee rivers were born here, high on the bald escarpment of the Australian Alps.

Smaller streams by the dozen ride the high country to the low—the Tumut, Mowamba, and Tooma rivers are three.

Within the area is also Canberra and, perhaps more important, Lake Burley Griffin, a water to be reckoned with when thinking of the best. It's a huge decorative sheet of water, commanding the respect of those who fish it.

Beginning in the northern parts of the Southern Tablelands district of Goulburn and Crookwell, the territory sweeps along to the Monaro plateau. Good roads carry traffic most of the year. The skiing enthusiasts arrive in time to greet the snow, and after them comes that weird and oddly assorted assembly known as the angling hoards.

So contrasting in character is this area that it's considered the most varied of all. The fishing here isn't so varied, however; usually it's great, consisting of good bags of exceptionally good fish.

## LAKES AND DAMS

### Burrinjuck Dam

A few years ago a magnificent brown trout of well over 8 kg fell to a trolling angler's lure. Introductions like this to a water are very rare indeed, so the Burrinjuck Dam must be something special. Patronised by anglers for most of the year, this water isn't a fool's paradise. Indeed, during the height of summer there's simply no way at all of securing a few fish, and often the experts themselves are brought rudely back to earth with only an empty bag to show for their efforts.

At other times, however, during the early part of spring, browns by the score will surrender themselves almost too willingly to whatever may be on the end of a line. Even primary-school children get into the act, throwing out a challenge to their betters who stand by in disgust at the way their favourite species of fish shows no caution at all. These suicidal tendencies quickly fade away and, within a week perhaps, the fishing returns to normal, to regain the respect of those who like to think they've earned their fish, having prepared for them in a dedicated manner.

Most of the bigger fish are taken on lures—but that's probably because these are most often used. Locally produced spoons compare favourably with those imported from overseas, but again, perhaps there's more of these hitting the water, thus accounting for such claims. The Baltic minnow appears to be the first choice of those who fish the water regularly, followed by the Pegron minnow, and the alpha sparkler. The Baltic minnow was specifically designed for the browns of Burrinjuck, and seems to be working a treat.

Bank fishing is almost as effective as fishing from a boat, and working a fast spinner close to the margins has much to recommend it.

A few big, battling browns are deceived by a bait, mostly a worm, but by far the greatest number submit to lures being trolled by the boats. Launching ramps are to be found at Hume Park, Good Hope, and the Burrinjuck Waters Park, where boats may also be hired.

Fed by the Murrumbidgee, the river below the dam has a water level that fluctuates often, depending on the demand for irrigation water down the river. Here some excellent fishing for reasonable brown trout is also to be had—these come on the bite whenever a good volume of water is discharged from the dam. Normally over-cautious fish suddenly become reckless enough to snatch at flies, lures and baits. At such times little skill is required to get more than a good bag of trout.

The Murrumbidgee waters immediately below the dam wall are now subject to permanent closure. Fishing pressure was brought to bear on the fish, which lacked all instincts of survival as they fought among themselves to get at whatever the angler offered, and the result was a set of conditions that could hardly be called sporting. Reports of enormous trout spotted by a team of divers working around the dam wall leave little doubt about the huge fish which still swim in this water, and which may one day fall victim to a beginner's lure, after rejecting out of suspicion those presented over a number of years by the expert. Such are the browns of Burrinjuck—suspicious and critical of our every move, until overwhelmed by that suicidal trait—then they're fair game for everyone! A recreation park, situated on the western shores of the lake, offers various activities for the family.

## Lake Burley Griffin

Named after the American architect Walter Burley Griffin who helped create the Canberra we see today, the lake itself adds much to the splendour of the city. Both exotic and native fish have been released in the lake for the dual purpose of producing some excellent fishing and as pest control. Creatures living in the water include shrimps, yabbies, different species of forage fish, water rats and a few platypuses. Imagine the turmoil that must take place beneath the surface as one species of wildlife feeds upon another. More variety comes with the birds, which help to retain something of a balance between all these creatures as they in turn arrive for their tucker.

Among the fish to be taken from the lake are brown and rainbow trout, brook trout, Murray cod, catfish and silver and golden perch, so there's plenty of variety. European carp have also appeared, to make their presence felt as they continue to increase in numbers and size. Fish of up to 9 kg have been caught, so it's safe to assume that some in the lake will probably be twice that size. At the moment, carp are causing some alarm in circles aware of the alleged damage they do to flourishing weed beds, and therefore indirectly to the other fish which share their environment. Another threat comes from the danger of contamination by the continuous flow of industrial and agricultural pollutants that may one day take its toll. At the moment, however, the threat is causing little concern, and the fishing continues to be of a high standard.

Fly-fishing is a popular method of getting amongst the trout and, in order to improve the standard of those perhaps not quite so proficient with the fly rod, the Canberra Anglers' Association gives free tuition on the foreshores of Lake Burley Griffin each year. Favoured flies are the coachman, muddler minnow and the hairwing. Some good sport is to be had when casting a fly at night.

Other acceptable ways of taking good fish include spinning with lures, and of course bait-fishing. With so many possible baits in the shape of live creatures living in the water, the problem of what to put on the hook shouldn't arise, provided they're obtainable at the time.

The big brown trout in this water are thought to feed extensively on the smaller carp which abound in such vast numbers. Trout (especially the browns) can be more cannibalistic than most fish, and will at times devour live fish of 200 g or more without the least hesitation. To prove the point, biologists regularly discover the scales and bones of baby carp in trout stomachs—carp because the carp are there to be had. If other tiny fish were available in such numbers then they'd undoubtedly go the same way—straight down a trout's gullet!

The Scrivener Dam was built in 1963 to arrest the waters of the Molonglo River to form Lake Burley Griffin. The river enters the lake 11 km east of this point. A natural picnicking area has been established just across the dam. Other picnic spots are found around the lake, and there are also boat launching ramps, for sailing craft only. Unfortunately for those who use them, no power boats are permitted on the lake.


## Canberra

Canberra and the Australian Capital Territory have some of the finest freshwater fishing in the land in the numerous streams and lakes that dot the area. Quite apart from the famed Lake Burley Griffin, which rates an individual entry, there are other still-waters containing much the same type of fish as are found in that lake.

Lake Ginninderra, in the centre of Belconnen, is one such water receiving the attention of the New South Wales Department of Fisheries in respect to fish stocking and breeding. Species used for experimental purposes include brook trout, brown and rainbow trout, catfish, silver and golden perch and Murray cod.

Like Burley Griffin, Lake Ginninderra supports more than enough life forms beneath the surface to satisfy even the most finicky of fish, which grow big and fat on such an abundant larder. Techniques for fishing this water are similar to those applicable to the better known water, and results are again similar, bearing in mind that the more regularly fished water must obviously produce the most fish.

While in more recent years the golden perch (also known as yellow-belly or callop) has improved considerably in its efforts to adapt to this new environment, it is the brown and rainbow trout that lead the field. Rainbows of 3 kg and browns of 4.5 kg have been recovered from Burley Griffin. From Lake Ginninderra have come an encouraging number of fish attaining a weight of up to 3 kg, so the future looks very bright indeed for the Canberra area freshwater fishing scene.

Now add the many rivers and streams that flow through the territory and the future looks brighter still! The Murrumbidgee is by far the biggest river, the others being considered little more than streams, or even creeks, for they creep quietly along attempting to hide the good fish from the prying eyes of the angler bent on removing some for the pot.

The Molonglo, Cotter, Gudgenby, Orroral and Paddys rivers, and also the Condor Creek, are very productive streams, and each drains into the Murrumbidgee. Each is basically a trout stream, though the mother river and the Molonglo support a few additional species that add to the spice of fishing them.

The effects of a long, wet winter leave many of these rivers and streams filled to capacity as they pick up speed and head for the Murrumbidgee, while in summer the reverse often applies. At such times the fish often head downstream to seek relief in the man-made dams or the deeper pools of the parent stream.

Fishing in each of the smaller streams is practised only by the spin-fisher and fly-fisher, because bait-fishing is strictly prohibited. They're pretty little fissures of water, containing enough small pockets of resistance in the shape of the trout that rise for a fly on the top to allow us to forgive their size. Paddys River in particular affords the novice an opportunity to practise with the fly rod, for although the trout are tiny, there's plenty of them to keep him busy as they rise to the top to test his skill.

The upper Molonglo River is so badly polluted from the wastage of the mines in the Captain Flat area that fish life of any kind can no longer survive in it. Nearer to Canberra the stream is met by the Queanbeyan River; it helps to purify the water enough to sustain a few species that have migrated from Lake Burley Griffin.

Below the lake the stream is subjected to occasional periods of drought, and it is also affected by a sewage plant that once released its effluence into the water at this point.

Paddys River is a tiny woodland stream, while the Condor Creek and Orroral River are much more heavily timbered. The Gudgenby River is larger than the others and carries better fish, although there appear to be fewer of them. The upper reaches of each riverlet travel through picture-book country and mountain catchments, that are virtually pollution-free. The angling worth of each varies, though all are patronised by those seeking out the trout.

Situated at altitudes of up to 2000 metres above sea level, the streams are just as the trout population prefer them. The fish will undoubtedly progress in size and number as they continue to acclimatise, and the streams may one day challenge the waters of the Snowy for their position at the top of the country's best trout waters.

## Googong Lake

This water, being the back-up lake behind the dam of Googong, is the newest addition to Canberra's fisheries. Opened to the angler for the first time in September 1979, the water is already winning a reputation for its trout fishing.

Situated within half-an-hour's reach of the majority of the city's fishermen, Googong Lake has been well received. Some controversy has blown up, however, over the fact that, after waiting impatiently for the dam to take shape, local anglers have now been informed that access to the water is restricted to the hours of 8 a.m. to 4 p.m. on weekdays, and up to 6 p.m. at weekends and holiday periods which, as we all know, is just about the worst time for trout fishing. It is hoped that shortly the authorities will see the folly of their ways and relent on this issue.

The dam is fed by the Queanbeyan River, which is itself a well respected trout stream. Apart from the river fish making their presence felt in the dam, rainbows, which make up the bulk of the catch, also are stocked in it. Some of these already are being taken to 2 kg, so the future of the water looks very bright indeed, and will doubtlessly be watched over with interest by the local fishing fraternity. Googong is ideally suited for those who wish to dabble a bait, fly or spoon after work in the evening—if only the ban can be lifted.

# QUEENSLAND

While most of Australia has been influenced considerably by the overseas angling scene, Queensland has stood grandly aloof and completely independent of other states, not to mention other countries. Whether this is a good thing is a matter of opinion. But the fact remains that the fish in Queensland are still as native as the Aborigines that angled for them long before white men ventured near the place.

Trout have never made their presence felt in Queensland, although a few have been reported from streams near the New South Wales border. But this is the land of more exotic species—the great barramundi, Australian bass, saratoga, sooty grunter and jungle perch. It's true that attempts have been made to introduce trout, but in each case the venture failed. But are they needed when there's the fighting barramundi to wrestle with?

Queensland covers an enormous area. It has been estimated that each square kilometre of space accommodates just one angler. So if it's elbow room you seek then here's the place to find it. Anglers from other states endure long journeys to fish up north—they consider the time and expense involved to be well worth it.

Fishing is open throughout the year, but fishermen up from the southern states tend to arrive in winter, when temperatures are cooler and bearable—the weather is usually far better than what they left behind. Despite the isolation of much of the Queensland territory, accommodation of many kinds is still to be had in all but the most barren areas where the angler must be reduced to sleeping in a tent. But at least he is on the spot when the fish choose to feed, be it at dawn, dusk, or throughout the night.

A four-wheel-drive vehicle may be needed to reach some of the way-out waters, and an ample supply of food and water is necessary in case things go wrong—it's not exactly unheard of for vehicles to gasp to a final standstill some distance from the nearest habitation.

When all things are geared to the rugged terrain you are ready for the unique fishing to be had up north—and it isn't all centred around the marlin boats. Netting in some places is beginning to have the effect on fishing that many foresaw years ago. The barramundi, although far from fished out, are now taking longer to find and are more effort to catch than was the case a decade ago.

Compared to other states, the intrusion of man upon nature is less evident here. The rivers, the valleys, the mountains and the streams are virtually untouched in places where industry has not yet made its claim. And it is right and proper that some regions, at least, are left unscathed by civilisation, if only to remind us of what we once had before adapting the land to our needs.

Those contemplating a visit up north would do well to confirm beforehand all bookings for accommodation and, where possible, to check out the areas to be fished so that all relevant local information can be assessed before arriving. It is small consolation to learn when you're there that the piece of water you intended to fish for barramundi has recently been netted out, or that you're unable to reach the water because of flooded tracks. Tourist Bureaux are listed at the back of this book, and other addresses are given at the end of the section 'Fishing for Barramundi'. Use them and save yourself from being disappointed.

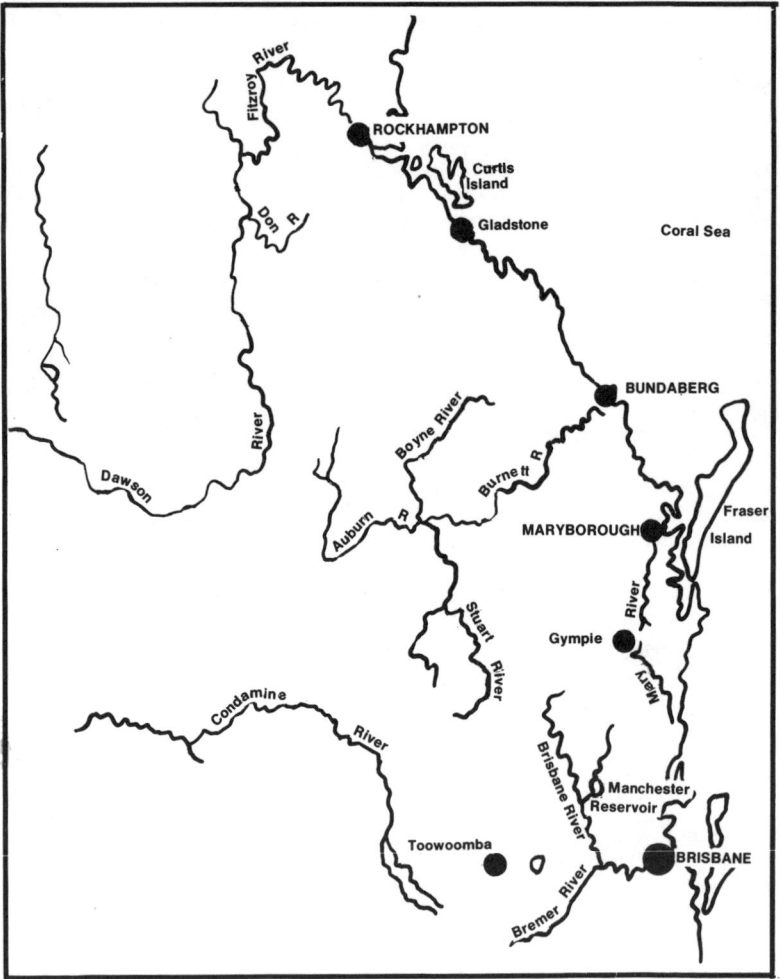

**QUEENSLAND**

# NATIVE FRESHWATER FISH

## Australian Perch

Better known to most as bass, the Australian perch (*Percalates colonorum*) also goes under the name of estuary perch. It's a widely distributed species, being found in most states. Reaching a maximum weight of about 5 kg it's not a particularly big fish, but is nonetheless highly respected for its sporting prowess. Today, a bass of a kilo is a worthy fish, and one of 2 kg is for some the fish of a lifetime in areas where their number and size has been reduced dramatically. Rarely departing from estuarine water, it is known to move downstream to breed in the estuaries during late winter or early spring. It is feared that continued construction of weirs and dams on coastal waters could eventually threaten the species.

## Barramundi

This is a highly prized fighting fish that is distributed from the Tropic of Capricorn north into the estuarine waters of Papua New Guinea. It spawns in and around the mouths of estuaries at the height of summer and, being a hermaphrodite species, the male fish turn into females as they mature. Barramundi are basically an estuary fish, rarely going beyond the tidal reaches of a river, so it is advisable to seek them well downstream. They are susceptible to all manner of lures, baits, and even to flies, and are the species most prized by anglers fortunate enough to be in a position to fish for them regularly. A barramundi grows to a possible 50 kg.

## Freshwater Mullet

This is not a very exciting fish and yet it can grow to more than 7 kg. Frequently encountered in the headwaters of the rivers and lagoons in south Queensland, it is particularly well established in the Noosa lakes and the attendant streams. Very little is known about this mullet which rarely reaches anywhere near its maximum size. It is considered to offer only moderate sport on the end of a line and is therefore not to be pursued enthusiastically.

## Grunter

'Grunter' is a name tagged to a family of perches, including the spangled perch, the black bream or sooty grunter of north Queensland and the silver perch. Relatively little is known about the Grunter family's breeding habits, although the spangled perch is believed to spawn at night. The grunter is quite widespread and almost abundant in some places—it may take up residence in rivers and dams and even in tiny billabongs. A small fish, often called jewel perch because of the flash of colour seen when first hooked, it feeds on small aquatic insects, crustaceans, molluscs and plant matter.

## Mangrove Jack

Technically a saltwater species, the mangrove jack does nevertheless penetrate freshwater. Distributed along the entire coast of Queensland, across the Gulf of Carpentaria to the Northern Territory, and to the northerly parts of Western Australia, the species relates best to the mangrove creeks and rivers of tropical Australia. It can reach a weight of about 10 kg, but the average fish taken will be less than half this size. It is applauded for its show of bravado when hooked, and also for its culinary qualities. It feeds mainly on small fish, prawns and crabs.

### Rifle- or Archer-fish
Mainly found in freshwater and water of low salinity, the rifle-fish is widely acclaimed for its unique talent—shooting insects at a range of more than a metre with a jet of water from its mouth. It feeds mostly on insects, shrimps and tiny fish. Although this species will accept an artificial fly, its size makes it hardly worth the effort. It is nonetheless an interesting little fish that is found in many aquariums.

Apart from the fish mentioned above, the visitor to Queensland will also find the opportunity to angle for what are normally termed the Murray fish. The golden perch or yellow-belly, for example, is found in the Fitzroy River system, that extends into south Queensland. The Murray cod will be there too, as will other fish from the south. But the visiting angler doesn't usually travel that distance to fish for cod. It's the giant barramundi that lures him away from his own territorial waters and, if he's done his homework well before leaving, he has every chance of succeeding.

### FISHING FOR BARRAMUNDI
To talk of a trip up north is to sound casual, giving no indication of the thought and preparation that must be expended on such a venture long before you actually hit the road. Gear must be checked and re-checked, new lines and lures must be purchased, and a finely detailed, localised map of the area to be visited must be studied even more closely than the Melbourne Cup runners' form.

But all this will be to no avail if you haven't studied with equal fanaticism the way you should go about getting the fish. Almost without exception you'll be in quest of the barramundi—but how's a joker from Melbourne to get amongst them if he hasn't a clue about how it's done? He often relies on nothing but mere chance, and therefore usually fails.

On the other hand, if a little research has been done, then he'll be in with a fighting chance. He'll learn, for example, that the best place to go is up in the Gulf Country or to Cape York, where conditions are more acceptable to the barramundi than around the east coast, although even there they may be encountered in the more isolated regions of Shoalwater Bay, between Rockhampton and Mackay. Barramundi are still present in some of the bigger rivers, such as the Fitzroy River and the Burdekin, although their numbers appear to be deteriorating each year.

Having selected the scene of battle with great care, it is a good policy to keep well downstream of any weirs which present a barrier for the barramundi. They've no spawning drive to urge them to surmount such formidable obstacles, so fish well below them. Lures and live fish baits are the accepted offerings, usually attached to heavy lines.

A new school of thought is now advocating lighter lines for barramundi. Even lines of a mere 2 kg in strength are being employed quite successfully by those who appreciate the limits of their gear in relation to the water being fished and the species involved.

Such a sporting gesture is to be applauded loudly. (It's about time the fish were given a fighting chance in this country!) But on the other hand we may have a situation that is hardly sporting at all. Fish taken on gossamer lines take a hell of a lot longer to subdue, and are therefore completely spent when finally brought to the net or gaff. Now that's all very well if the fish is to be killed there and then, but happily more and more anglers are releasing a fair portion of the fish they take. So what chance of recovery have those that are completely exhausted? Precious little, I would think.

There's also the greater risk of fish finding the snags more easily when on the end of a light line, and of then breaking off, becoming hopelessly entangled in a mesh of nylon to suffer a prolonged and agonising death. Yet it must still be considered a step in the right direction to tempt them on more reasonable lines—not to promote points in a contest, but merely to give our quarry an even chance to pit its wits against ours.

Lure-fishing is the method most rigidly adhered to when barramundi are sought—and not without good reason. The species complies perfectly with everyone's idea of what fishing with lures is all about. Barramundi literally throw themselves at the lures at times to afford us an exhilarating experience, add to that their usual size, and they're well on the way to providing superfishing!

Barramundi show a marked preference for relatively shallow water, a point to keep in mind when selecting a lure to tempt them with, as some lures are designed to be fished deep while others function best at mid-water. Indeed, some are even fashioned to be worked right on the surface, and that's looking at the most basic of lures and lure-fishing.

In fact, everything with a hook attached is a lure, be it a bait, fly or spinner. But in fishermen's language a lure is usually an imitation fish made of wood, rubber or some other material. Spinners are often referred to as lures in Australia, while overseas they're normally classified as spoons. But in America, where lure-fishing really began, the term 'plugs' is used. It must be stressed that the kind of lure used for barramundi is normally imitation fish.

To impart an enticing movement to the lure is an art in itself, although many anglers believe that, because the lure has been made to resemble a fish, there's nothing else involved—you simply chuck out the thing and then wind it back in. Nothing could be further from the truth. It's the action put into the lure that does the trick—an action developed over a number of years.

That isn't to say that because an angler has never used a lure before, he isn't in with a chance. He will, however, be in a better position once he's gained more experience—learned about what each kind can do under certain conditions, and is able to tell at a glance which kind is most likely to succeed no matter what the conditions may be.

Colour, shape and size will also depend on many factors that only the angler himself can assess while actually fishing but for barramundi generally a lure that floats or one that dives not too far beneath the surface is the most popular. These are worked in combination with bait-casting gear, i.e. a revolving-drum-type reel and a short flexible rod with enough stick to flick the lure out.

The wands that the Americans first produced for the job were so supple that they could actually be tied in knots. But what control they'd have over a fish is anyone's guess. Some anglers tackle the barramundi with threadline or spinning reels, but these must lack some of the control needed for a fish that leaves us shaking by the way it leaps all over the place and then takes off for the distant horizon.

Clear banks are necessary for bait-casting, and since barramundi haunts are normally found in waters that are anything but clear, a boat is absolutely essential, except perhaps where the rivers widen downstream. The bait-fisher, however, can often manage from the bank, and many fine specimens are caught on live fish that are allowed to roam around freely until taken.

At night especially a bait will take fish, for the kind we seek is really a nocturnal feeder, even though good numbers are taken during the day. At dusk the bait-caster may continue to work his lure from the boat, but it's not the beginner's scene. Nor are saltwater flies for the beginner. Extremely skilled hands are required to work them effectively around the boulders and snag-ridden swims that are so typical of barramundi water, and each fish taken in this manner calls for a round at the bar.

Like most other fish, barramundi are susceptible to the tread of the angler's foot, whether it be encased in leather or not. The bank-fisher in particular must be cautious in his approach, for he will be nearer the quarry. Yet the boat too, must be handled carefully, stealthily, so as not to put the fish down. An old, flat-bottomed wooden punt makes a better barra boat than those noisy, aluminium craft used these days—but the old punt is no longer a part of the everyday scene.

Barramundi country really begins at the Mary River, a few hundred kilometres north of Brisbane, and some barra-fishers claim that the fish are as big and as numerous here as they are way up north. That's still quite a journey for most folks. But if you're bent on going, then prepare for the trip well in advance. Leave nothing to chance and you may return with a few barramundi.

### A Few Useful Addresses
*Queensland Conservation Council:* 147 Ann Street, Brisbane 4000; *Queensland Fisheries Service:* 138 Albert Street, Brisbane 4000; and *Queensland Amateur Fishing Clubs Association:* 39 Parooba Avenue, Camp Hill, 4152.

### RIVERS AND DAMS
### Brisbane River
This river is badly polluted by the drainage from the city's industry and the river traffic that is heavy for most of the year. But there's still some decent fishing to be had in parts. Mostly estuary species are to be found here, particularly near the mouth of the river, where bream, whiting, flathead and even a few big mulloway congregate. Tiny jewfish or river perch enter the Brisbane River in early winter and stay until spring. They're very keen on yabbies, worms and prawns. Accepted bream hot spots are established at the Abattoir, Hamilton walls and White Island. The river rises in the Brisbane-Cooyar Range and flows south-east through rich agricultural country to Moreton Bay. The Brisbane River was discovered by a couple of runaway convicts in 1823! It is of little interest to the freshwater fisherman.

## Daintree River

Recognised as one of the prettiest little tropical streams in the country, the Daintree River is found after an hour's drive north of Cairns. The tiny township of Daintree is situated 24 km above the mouth of the river. Jungle perch abound in the river and nearby creeks. The Stewart Creek tributary is particularly favoured for the species. They're not very big fish but give some sport when taken on lures. Elsewhere the jungle perch is said to be dying out, but hopefully that won't happen here. Much of the terrain in the area of the Daintree River is virtually untouched, and huge crocodiles are sometimes present. Some delightful rainforest streams exist near Cooktown to offer more jungle perch fishing, and eel-tail catfish are also present.

## Endeavour River

Located in the region of Cooktown, the Endeavour River is where Captain Cook's craft ended up after coming to grief on the reefs off Cape Tribulation. It's a difficult 340-km journey from Cairns. The roads are rough and rugged for most of the way, treacherous when wet weather causes the mountain streams to rise and sometimes flood the tracks, and are unsuitable for towing caravans or boats. At the height of the season, however, many cars pass through the region. A new road should by now have been completed along the coast to ease the situation. The Endeavour is a good river to fish. Nearby is the Annam River, and both carry barramundi, mangrove jacks, grunter and threadfin salmon.

## Gregory River

This northern Queensland water is comparable in beauty to that anywhere. Flowing west to the Gulf of Carpentaria, its upper reaches support a good head of sooty grunter, some archer-fish, fork-tail catfish and other kinds of fish. They're usually quite small, but are great fun to catch nevertheless. In the lower reaches some battling barramundi are to be had. The lesser known saratoga will also appear in some adjacent creeks.

The river travels in much the same direction as the equally beautiful O'Shanassy River, which is similar in character to it. Near the headwaters to both is yet another river, the Georgina, which carries mainly Murray fish, such as the golden and silver perch. The Georgina, however, sets off in a southerly direction, which probably explains why it yields an entirely different species. Most of the land here is used for pastoral purposes and permission must be sought before wetting a line. But don't let that stop you. A request to fish, put in the right manner, will almost invariably be granted.

## Mitchell River

The Mitchell River at Cape York is claimed to be one of the biggest tributary systems in the land. The annual drain-off from the wet season is apt to create the most serious flooding up north. Not a great fish water, it nevertheless produces some good sport. In the upper reaches of some tributaries there are freshwater grunter, or black bream, to catch, along with some catfish. The Lynd, Alice, Walsh and Palmer are the most popular. Unfortunately barramundi rarely venture this far inland, although there's always a chance. The river is continually affected by the dry season, running almost empty at times, and the fish then gather in whatever deep pools remain.

**Other Waters**

Among the other waters worth mentioning is the Johnstone River and nearby streams at Innisfail, where a fair number of barramundi are taken each year. Mangrove jack and threadfin salmon also exist here. The Tinaroo Dam on the Barron River also deserves a try. It affords the visitor a great deal of space for boating and fishing. Noted for the good stock of sleepy cod it contains, the dam is a popular venue. Fork-tail catfish, black bream, and some spirited spangled perch add much to the potential catch here. The dam is about 7 km from the tiny township of Atherton.

The Mary River at Maryborough contains Murray cod and yellow-belly in the freshwater reaches, and is also accepted as the southerly limit of barramundi. The township of Maryborough is well geared to coping with the stream of tourists who drop in at the height of the fishing season.

In the south-east generally we find a number of smaller rivers and dams, most of which carry bass, Murray cod, yellow-belly, mullet, spangled perch, catfish, mangrove jack, saratoga, and that wonderfully sporting fish, the tarpon. Among these waters are the Currumbin, Tallebudgera and Mudgeeraba creeks, running north along with the Albert, Logan, Nerang and Coomera rivers. A series of small dams at the headwaters of these streams caters for the Gold Coast region.

Connecting with the Brisbane River are streams like the Lockyer and Bremer, that serve to drain the western slopes of the Great Divide. The Manchester, Somerset, Atkinson and Moogerah dams act as a link in the entire system. Another dam recently completed is known as the North Pine Dam, and is one of the largest in the area.

Many other waters drift across the south-east, and are somewhat underrated as fisheries, which is a pity because they offer some challenge to the freshwater scene in Queensland. The bass especially have a huge following, particularly among the locals who tempt them on worms, crickets, and other such natural baits, although some prefer to tangle with them on lures. But in warm weather, when the insects are out in force, it goes without saying that one of these on a hook has simply got to be tried.

The mullet fishing is something of a farce—it is akin to the schoolboy-with-the-bent-pin approach— hardly to be taken seriously by those with a more sophisticated outlook. Yet it must be grand fun nonetheless, pursued as it is more by the locals than the tourist. These freshwater mullet are abundant in the upper reaches of the Brisbane River and tributaries.

The mangrove jack is an obliging little fish—absolutely full of fight and ready to have a go at whatever's on the end of the line. Very much a mid-summer species, they're never happier than when playing about in the mangroves, as their name suggests. They are an aggressive breed, snapping viciously at anything darting before their eyes and, if it happens to contain a hook, then a lively struggle is assured.

Tarpon are more readily appreciated for their sporting worth, and more widely acclaimed for it. They're not an easy fish to trick into taking a lure and must therefore be approached with all the cunning the angler possesses. Delicate lines affixed to tiny lures can hardly be expected to contain them, yet that's the advice given to those who seek them. They're a sensitive species offering a lot of thrilling moments, particularly when a school of smaller fish is encountered, but the better ones demand the kind of knowledge and skill that is sadly lacking in most who wield a wand.

On the Mary River at Gympie, north of Brisbane, a hatchery geared to breeding golden perch (yellow-belly) and barramundi is by now well established; it is expected to yield 20 000 perch and 2000 barramundi each year. Such steps have been taken to ensure that fears that the species could become extinct can never materialise. Let's wish those involved every success, and hope that similar hatcheries in other states turn their attention to the breeding and distribution of Murray species, and let the trout take second billing for a change. We do need the trout, particularly in the south where it thrives so well, but a bit of variety wouldn't go amiss!

## THE GULF COUNTRY

What magic that name conjures up in the minds of we would-be adventurers! Not without good reason either, because the fishing can be out of this world, which it nigh is anyway, up there. But those keen to make the trip should be aware of the best time to go and the rivers to fish. They should also study the terrain they're entering before chucking the gear in the back and heading off for parts unknown.

The time to make the trip is at the end of March, when, hopefully, the wet season is at an end. To travel before then may mean you won't get through, although newly built roads in some areas do ease the strain a bit. From Cairns a reasonable road via Croydon will lead you to some fine fishing in the gulf country, as will the Lynd Highway from Townsville, via Charters Towers to Georgetown, then from Croydon to Normanton.

From Julia Creek and Clohcurry to Normanton is a reasonably comfortable drive, as is the journey from the turn-off at Donors Hill to Augustus Downs and then to Burketown. The trip from Mount Isa to Normanton via Cloncurry is much the same, although that hasn't always been the case. To get to Burketown from Mount Isa, travel along the Barkly Highway for about an hour via Gregory Downs and you're there. Burketown makes an excellent base for fishing the estuaries of the Albert, Nicholson and Leichhardt rivers. But on the way in, why not give it a try in the Gregory River, 38 km south of the Downs? The river flows alongside the road, and is well noted for its fishing.

From Burketown to Borroloola calls for the use of a four-wheel-drive job in the dry season, and probably a boat in the wet. But there's some fine fishing up that way in the rivers and creeks from Wollogorang onwards, if you can make it.

Normanton seems more civilised than Burketown, with some extra-good fishing for barramundi, catfish and bream at Glenore Bar, Walkers Creek and other waters within reach of the town. But Karumba is the main angling centre on the gulf, being established right on the estuary of the Norman River. A few facilities here in terms of camping and boat-hire make it the best region to head for, although confirmation should be made in advance.

Among the different species to be expected in and around the estuary are the following: threadfin salmon, white salmon, catfish, mulloway, queenfish, mangrove jacks, sawfish, sharks and rays of all kinds, bream, and of course, our main interest, the barramundi. Now that's a big enough selection of fish for any water—and any angler, unless he's particularly difficult to please—and it gives some idea of why a fortunate few head up-country at enormous expense to fish the gulf country. The roads these days make the long journey a little easier to bear, but the forever rising cost of fuel and necessities have succeeded magnificently in putting the gulf country further out of reach to many.

## SOUTH AUSTRALIA

# SOUTH AUSTRALIA

In South Australia there is a dearth of freshwater lakes and streams. This is due mainly to the comparatively low rainfall of the region, and a character that doesn't lend itself well to the creation and maintenance of natural freshwater basins. It follows that little inland fishing is available in the state. The Murray River caters for the vast majority of anglers who prefer freshwater to saltwater fishing, and fortunately the Murray is always ready to oblige them.

Very much a water of the summer season, the Murray River normally fishes best from November to April and, as with most waters, early morning, late afternoon and evening will produce the finest results. Night fishing offers opportunities of getting into some excellent Murray cod; it is at such times that the cod specialist will be found waiting for the fish to leave their lairs to feed.

When there is a fluctuation of the water level before or after a flood peak is the time held as the most promising of all to fish; it also aids the natural breeding process of the fish; therein ensuring a good stock of fish for the future. No licence is necessary to take the fish in South Australia, but since access to the riverside is often through private property, permission should be sought before venturing further. There is also a heavy penalty for the angler found with live carp in his possession; the European species has been declared a noxious fish. A few trout are found in the Murray, but generally these are sought in the streams that are more to their liking.

## MURRAY RIVER

From its source on the southern side of the Snowy Mountains in New South Wales, the Murray heads for the South Australian coast 2570 kilometres away. Joined by the Darling, Murrumbidgee, Lachlan and Goulburn rivers, the waters of the Murray directly and indirectly flow into several states; when added together they give a grand total of 5285 kilometres for the Murray-Darling system, making it one of the largest of its kind in the world.

The Murray River (and to a lesser degree its tributaries) is the last remaining stronghold of some species of fish unique to this land—the indigenous species, so rapidly becoming rare now in the inland waterways, having been ousted from their rightful position over the years by fish originally bred in foreign parts. The Murray cod, reputed to reach a weight of 90 kg, making it the largest of our freshwater fish, is now taken in inferior numbers and size from the pathetic remains of what was once the vast range of their natural habitat. The Macquarie perch, always super-sensitively shy of the angler's bait, now borders on extinction in regions where our forefathers fished specifically for this species. The golden perch or callop, the catfish, the silver perch and trout cod are disappearing. The trout cod was capable of attaining a weight of 16 kg when encountered, as it commonly was, in the lower reaches of the Murray, particularly near Yarrawonga; but that was thirty or so years ago. The trout cod is a rarity there now; where have they all gone?

All of these species once filtrated the waters of many states via the River Murray and its tributaries in worthwhile numbers; now they cause something of a sensation when they are taken even from parts of the

Murray proper—proof enough of their scarcity. From an angling point of view, perhaps the introduction of some fish previously alien to our waters was a step in the right direction, for they replaced a few indigenous species offering little if any challenge at all on the end of a line. The river blackfish (commonly known as slippery) particularly comes to mind here, for its sporting potential is practically nil. But the biologist sees the situation in a different light. The nature of his work allows him to see ahead of us, and the sight he visualises isn't a pretty one.

The alarming rate at which native species of many kinds are disappearing from the great Australian outdoors is most depressing indeed. The blackfish, for example, has no known genetically related species anywhere in the world. Yet sadly the blackfish is dying out fast! If we're at all concerned about their diminishing numbers it's absolutely imperative that any caught be returned to the water with the least possible harm and delay—and that applies to other fish becoming rare in our lakes, rivers and streams.

It is undoubtedly fortunate for those who reside in South Australia that the Murray River isn't completely barren of native fish, otherwise they'd have nothing but European carp and redfin to tackle. The carp are now, of course, officially classified as a noxious species, yet they offer some kind of sport when all else fails to oblige us. It can be said with some honesty that if it weren't for the carp most anglers on certain parts of the Murray would end the day fishless—but if the carp hadn't been put there such a situation wouldn't exist, perhaps.

The carp are obviously here to stay, despite repeated attempts to be rid of the so-called vermin, so we may as well approach their haunts as seriously as those of any other species, and attempt to catch them in a serious manner. There are those who believe that carp fishing is a pastime for children, requiring no skill at all; up to a point this appears true, but why aren't the really big fish being taken?

Overseas, carp are held in high esteem, and they are sought with the dedication reserved in Australia for trout. Indeed, the carp elsewhere really is an opponent worthy of pursuit by even the best of anglers. Cunning, sensitive to the lightest drag and the most innocent of smells, its tag of being the wily carp was put there for good reason. Yet in Australia we seem almost to have a different species, which really confuses the issue. Medium-sized fish can be taken almost without our trying, as they gulp down baits intended for other fish. Perhaps they do this because their sheer weight in numbers leaves them no option but to grab whatever morsel presents itself before another of their kind reaches the prize first. As well, even an average-sized carp is big compared to most native species. So, with the phenomenal population explosion of the species here in Australia (which incidentally isn't the accepted norm), we have a situation where huge numbers of naturally large fish are competing for a feed in an environment not equipped to support them. It's an interesting theory at least that explains the devil-may-care manner in which they form a queue to become rotting matter on the banks of our rivers and dams—a sad ending to what some believe to be a real sporting fish in its true domain, a challenger with a worthy gauntlet to drop at our feet.

Whatever your personal feelings towards European carp, you'll find more than enough in the Murray, especially where it creeps through South Australia. The river is 20 million years old. Along its banks have sprung up many townships, some with much to offer the visitor. Since the Murray is frequented not merely for the fishing but also for holidays, perhaps with the family, it is well to know that for most of its length the waterside townships are there to pamper the angler and to make his visit a memorable one.

Where to stay on the Murray is very much a personal choice, determined among other things by what you wish to do when not fishing. Many towns have places of interest that add to the joy of being there. Each has facilities for boat-hire also—the best way to see the Murray is actually being afloat on her. Growing numbers of holiday-makers each summer leave the banks at one point and work their way slowly along to other ports-of-call, perhaps pitching a tent at night under the nearby red gums and then pushing off again after breakfast. That is the finest way to get to know the Murray, and must be recommended to those capable of roughing it a bit. Snakes can be a nuisance at times; however, they're not a problem peculiar to the banks of the Murray.

Along the Murray River in South Australia are to be found Public Fishing Reserves, marked at various points by yellow arrow signs, where the amateur fisherman can angle to his heart's content without being plagued by the presence of his professional counterpart. The lower regions of the Murray appear to be more able to deal with the needs of the influx of anglers each summer, when the fishing is at its peak. Goolwa, Mannum, and Murray Bridge are three of the better locations, offering good sport and first-class facilities in accommodation and boat-hire. Murray cod, callop, redfin, perch, catfish, bream and European carp are the species listed as being available here for the angler's enjoyment, although it must be stressed again that the native Murray fish are nowhere near as plentiful as perhaps some travel agents would have us believe. Yet they do tend to gather in small shoals, so more than just the odd fish might be expected when they are located. The task of finding them in the first place may well be the most difficult part of all, but that's the case with any kind of fishing!

Baits used must depend mainly on the season and locality. Shrimps and worms are to be had close to the banks, and are claimed to be excellent for the carp, redfin and callop, although the Murray cod needs a more tempting mouthful to arouse it from the depths of its slumber on the river bed. A Flopy lure or spinner will shift it, and at the same time account for the callop or redfin. A long-standing although unfortunate bit of advice often given is to use line as thick as rope to handle the cod. As this must knock the hell out of them before they've moved even a metre, and as the majority of cod taken are more likely to be nearer 10 kg than the widely acclaimed 90 kg, it is suggested instead that the would-be cod-clobberer select a line that's light enough to give him some sport, rather than heavy enough to deal with some mythical monster that ruled the mainflow a century ago . . .

The normal-size cod haunt the deeper runs alongside the steep banks, but often venture to where the deeper water joins the shallows, probably to hunt the baby fish there. Bends in the river also warrant some added attention. The carp are more often found in the backwaters, where the deep sluggish flow suits them better. These too can afford us some splendid sport on lines not designed for securing the huge riverboats that were once so much a part of the scene here. (Cruises may still be had on the Murray, by the way, passing away a few pleasant hours in ideal country, and perhaps regaining for a spell some of the atmosphere of an era now past. The kids will enjoy it anyhow, so why not give them a treat!)

To dismiss the Murray is to forget about freshwater fishing altogether in South Australia, there being no other place worthy of comment. There are a few tiny streams, some of which contain some surprisingly big trout, considering the waters they come from. One such river is the Onkaparinga, situated in the Adelaide Hills. From here, a certain angler residing at West Croydon is forever pulling out trout big enough to make those Eucumbene fish blush. Many trout to almost 6 kg have come this fellow's way, and his picture with them in the local papers is beginning to be a regular feature. Yet I've been informed by a reliable source that fishing this particular water is difficult because of its enclosure within private land.

Largely due to the lack of suitable streams for the venture, acclimatisation attempts to establish reasonable trout fisheries as in other states have failed most miserably in South Australia. Within the city of Adelaide, the Torrens Gorge is perhaps one of the finest trout fishing regions in the state. Another is the Finnis River, which flows down the Adelaide Hills to empty into Lake Alexandrina. Dozens of other streams have been regularly stocked with trout by the Acclimatisation Society of Adelaide, and also by the South Australian Fly Fishers' Association, but compared to other states the fishing isn't very successful. The Light River produces some excellent sport with exceptionally large rainbows and browns, compared to the size of the normal run of fish in the area, and much the same can be said for the Para and Wakefield rivers. It's simply a pity that the many other streams in the state aren't nearly as productive.

The trout anglers of South Australia are reading their morning newspapers with more fervour than normal these days, because there's a strong possibility that in the foreseeable future the reservoirs in that state will be opening their gates to allow the hordes of fishing fanatics to enter. The question of fishing the dams was raised some time ago but the powers-that-be have taken their time about mulling over the matter— shifting it to the bottom of the agenda when it should rightfully be nearer the top.

At the moment these waters are to be used only for 'passive recreation', (it conjures up all manner of thoughts!)—which apparently means sightseeing and picnicking. But don't fret—somebody has let it be known that fishermen also reside in South Australia, and are also entitled to consideration. So it may well be that shortly freshwater fishing in this state may get a badly needed boost.

Of the six large reservoirs within easy reach of Adelaide, the South Para Reservoir is expected to be the first to serve the angler's needs; hopefully the remainder will soon follow suit. The potential of these waters has been likened to that found in Lakes Pedder and Gordon of Tasmania, so it's an opportunity well worth fighting for. Victoria has twenty-two reservoirs, many of them open to fishing and some even to boating, so why should those in other states be closed?

## RIVERSIDE TOWNSHIPS

Most of the fishing on the Murray River is done in and around one of the many towns that have grown up alongside the water. Any of those mentioned below can serve as the angler's base.

### Barmera

Delightful riverside scenery is to be found here, with exotic forms of birdlife to add to the over-all picture. Boat ramps and barbecue areas are available for the angler's convenience. Lake Bonney nearby is geared for all kinds of water sports, including sailing, water-skiing, speedboat racing and fishing, if you're prepared to try your luck amidst all that disturbance. Picnics and barbecues can also be enjoyed at Apex Park on the eastern foreshore. Pioneer Park, facing the police station, may be worth a visit to see the implements used by the early settlers. The display includes a huge Fowler engine.

### Berri

A camping ground and picnic area are situated near the lock just a short drive off the highway, with orchards and vineyards to be passed on the way. The river front at Martins Bend is blessed with a recreation area popular for picnics and barbecues. An excellent boat ramp is nearby. Another picnic and fishing spot can be found at Katarapko Creek, just 12 km from the centre of town. A look-out tower at Fiedler Street offers the chance of taking some great panoramic photographs of the town and the river. It is a favourite reach of the Murray for fishing and yabbying.

### Loxton

Loxton is of historical interest, as the village of Loxton is founded on the river near the site of William Loxton's old log cabin and the pepper tree he planted there. A museum contains ancient farming tools together with farm buildings, a railway station and vintage cars. Habels Bend on the river front has a camping and picnicking ground, plus a boat ramp. But of more interest to the angler will be the fish hatchery close to the river.

### Renmark

The recreation park at Plushs Bend is one of the more popular venues for fishing, camping, swimming and boating. Bredl's Reptile Park and Zoo boasts of having one of the largest collections of snakes in the country (as if we didn't see enough along by the water when we're fishing!) including such notorious killers as the taipan, death adder, tiger snake and python; even some crocodiles are there to add to our fear. The park is open daily. Based in the area is the cruise ship *Murray Explorer* that has room for 138 passengers. Renmark is considered to be the bottom of the top end of the Murray.

### Waikerie

Holder Bend Reserve is a popular resort for water-skiing and picnicking, but it hardly appears to be the place to wet a line. Birdwatching can be enjoyed on Harts Lagoon. A kangaroo park is found at Waikerie adjacent to the riverside, where the grass-covered banks make it an ideal place to have a picnic or barbecue. Waikerie is known overseas for the glider flying that takes place in the area. Its Aboriginal name means 'many wings'!

## HOLIDAYS AFLOAT

At Berri, Loxton and Renmark a fleet of houseboats is available for hire, allowing the angler and his entire family the freedom of Huckleberry Finn in this rich, rural, riverland setting. The vessels have a top speed of six to eight knots, and a range to take them well up or down the river. Each is equipped with all the comforts of home. They vary in size from four to ten berths, and are thoroughly recommended to those who feel they must get away from it all for a time. Hiring commences at 2 p.m. on the first day and terminates at 9 a.m. on the last, unless otherwise arranged. It is advisable to book well in advance.

*Berri:* Swan; 6/8/10-berth vessels, minimum hire 3 to 5 days (seasonal); linen may be hired.

*Loxton:* Barinya; 8/10-berth, minimum hire 3 days; linen included in hire.

*Renmark:* Liba Liba; deluxe vessels of varying sizes, able to sleep 4 to 10 persons, minimum hire 2 days; all linen included (school holiday surcharge applicable).

Many other boats may be booked through the Renmark Tourist Office. More details relating to the hiring of houseboats may be had from the South Australian Government Tourist Bureau in your nearest city, where literature is available and bookings can be arranged.

### Day Cruises

Day cruises on the Murray River can be had on the MV *Pelican*, which departs from the Lake Bonney Motel, Barmera, at 10 a.m. on Sundays and public holidays. The *Pelican* cruises across Lake Bonney to Chambers Creek, where numerous species of birdlife can be studied at close quarters. Bookings may be made at the Barmera Tourist Office.

As well, there is the MV *Barrangul*, which departs Wednesdays, Sundays and public holidays; also daily throughout school holidays from the Renmark Wharf at 2 p.m. Dinner cruises are planned for Fridays and Saturdays. Licensed refreshments and afternoon tea are available. Bookings can be made at Riverland tourist offices. Both vessels are available for private hire. Other cruise craft depart from Goolwa, Murray Bridge, and from Mannum.

## LOWER MURRAY NATIONAL PARKS AND RESERVES

Few places can be blessed with such a concentration of parks and reservation areas as those found on the lower reaches of the River Murray, some of which are noted below for those who wish to combine their fishing with a walk through nature's realm.

### Coorong National Park

This consists of an area 106 km in length, embracing Younghusband Peninsula across Coorong Lake to Princes Highway south of Salt Creek. Unique geology is found in this region which covers 37 000 hectares of maritime sand dune vegetation. Wombats and waterbirds of many descriptions add much to the scenery, including pelicans, ducks and several species of terns. Cars are not permitted on Younghusband

Peninsula, with the exception of ocean beach which requires the service of four-wheel-drive vehicles.

### Long Island Recreation Park
This is located in the Murray River south of Murray Bridge, from where access by boat is made. Beautifully scenic with willows and red gum trees, it is ideal for bird watching and photographing. Well worth the effort of a visit.

### Mud Island Game Reserve
Much better than its name implies, the game reserve does in fact consist of ten tiny islands in Lake Alexandrina, covering a total of 138 hectares. Reached by boat from Clayton or Point Sturt, the area is worth a trip if only to check it out for the duck shooting permitted here in season. Large reed beds create an environment ideally suited to the waterbirds that inhabit this terrain in vast numbers.

### Pooginook Conservation Park
Further along the river and 12 km north-east of Waikerie is the Pooginook Conservation Park, which allows you to see wildlife in many forms, including western grey kangaroos, echidnes, emus, Mallee fowl and hairy-nosed wombats. The park is reached from the Morgan–Barmera Highway.

### Whites Dam Conservation Park
Nine kilometres north-west of Morgan is where this park is located, containing western grey and red kangaroos and other creatures in the black oak woodland. Included in the park is part of the old Morgan–Burra travelling stock route. The entrance to the area will be found along the Morgan–Burra Road. The park covers 911 hectares.

### Wilabalangaloo National Trust Reserve
Open daily except Tuesdays and Fridays. A good place for a picnic with barbecue facilities available. Just 3 km along on Sturt Highway, north of Berri, the reserve has picturesque walking tracks through an area filled with different species of both flora and fauna. Some added interest can be gained by visiting the museum in the reserve.

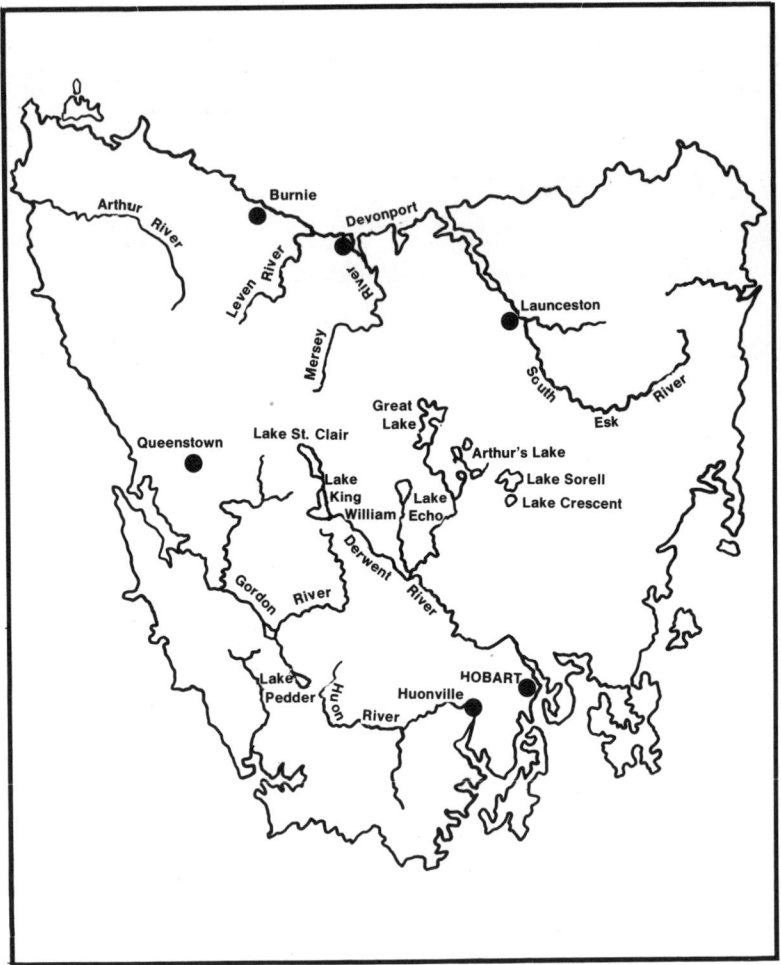

**TASMANIA**

# TASMANIA

Across Bass Strait south-east of the Australian mainland lies a tiny island called Tasmania, once renowned for the devil that stalked the undergrowth but now becoming famous world-wide for the magnificent trout that are being taken with almost monotonous regularity. We're all aware of them because barely a month passes without some fishing scribe showing off his catch of Tasmanian trout within the pages of an angling magazine—whacking great fish that are difficult to accept as the real thing. But they're the genuine article all right, and they invariably come from Lake Pedder.

Surprisingly, though, Pedder was once a tiny, picturesque glacial lake, until enlarged in the early 1970s by the Serpentine River being dammed, and a section of the Huon River being allowed in; we all know it's an enormous sheet of water now, often described as an inland sea. But of course, Pedder isn't the only lake in Tasmania—there are thousands there—or at least hundreds.

Lake Pedder is ahead of them all as a trout fishery. It is also the most popular, so why shouldn't many of the other waters do as well, if not better, if they were fished as often? For each of the noted rivers and lakes there must be an equal number unheard of by those on the mainland.

Because Pedder's fish became publicised, the economics of the situation were studied so that today package holidays to Pedder and other waters are a standing practice, some of the few of their kind. Promotion is now in full swing to lure the trout-fisher from all points of the globe to sample the fishing, and various waters are being developed for the sole purpose of enticing the tourist.

Catering for the last of the big spenders is big business, but will the day dawn when the little bloke with his little wage packet can't get a look in? That mustn't be allowed to happen, or we'll have a situation such as exists in Scotland, where the gentry still have their gillies to row them to the salmon while the humble serfs make do with sardines.

Some attempt at development is needed for us to be able to get to the scene, for it brings transport and accommodation. Caravan parks, car- and boat-hire are now readily available for those bent on an expedition to the lakes of Tasmania, and such facilities weren't widespread ten years ago. It's a comforting thought to know that when we arrive we'll be well looked after.

Let's not forget the waters other than Lake Pedder though: Lake Sorell, Penstock Lagoon, the Great Lake and the Western Lakes, the Macquarie River and Brumbys Creek. There are so many to choose from, and each is well stocked with trout—big trout, that make those from the Snowy Mountains look like so many tiddlers.

Not every lake on this fantastic island produces monster trout. Some can average at best a kilo, while others manage fish that are usually twice that size, which aren't to be sniffed at. Yet we go to Tasmania to get ourselves a giant. Most of the better known waters are quite capable of producing fish of 5 kg or more, and not a year passes without one or the other proving it.

Way back in 1875 a 10 kg hen fish was trapped by the local authorities and stripped of her eggs; these were used to stock a number of waters. So big trout are not exactly new to Tasmania; there are simply more of them now, getting bigger and receiving the publicity due them.

In 1975 four trout from individual waters each weighed over 8 kg. From Lake Crescent in 1973 came a huge fish estimated to be 14.5 kg; when cleaned it was officially weighed in at 12 kg. The biggest claimed from Lake Pedder was taken in January 1980 on a minnow lure by Launceston angler Jim Brown, and weighed 11.4 kg. So is it any wonder then that some anglers believe that Tasmania is stealing the limelight from New Zealand as the finest trout-fishing resort in the world?

Probably for those in the south a trip over to Tasmania would be no more expensive than a visit to Lake Eucumbene, especially if a group of four or five anglers were to share the expense; but as always it makes great sense to learn all you can about the place and the fishing before setting off half-cocked. On Pedder, for instance, bait-fishing is not allowed, and brown trout waters close late April or early May each year.

Because of the Tasmanian hydro-electric scheme many new and enormous waters have been created for our use, which we acknowledge with due solemnity. Yet without them Tasmania would still have a great deal to offer. Hundreds of lakes, lagoons and rivers exist more than 1000 metres above sea level that are cool, clean, and completely unpolluted. In the trout's lingo this is home sweet home—the ideal environment for a species that demands the best. It's not incidental that trout are invariably found in the most crystalline of streams, or in the purest of still waters—they like it that way, and need it to survive. And survive they do quite remarkably in the Tasmanian waters, as has been proven time and again.

The story goes that on 4 May 1864 the local supervisor of the Plenty Salmon Ponds was checking out a newly arrived batch of ova shipped over from Britain when he noticed that one egg had been shattered open and inside could be seen a lively trout alvin; that resulted in the first trout fishery in the Southern Hemisphere. It's a nice tale anyway, and it is a fact that from the Plenty Salmon Ponds each state in Australia, as well as New Zealand, received its first batch of trout.

Tasmania is a rugged place, with weather that has to be watched and allowed for at times. Some of the bigger lakes can be most unkind in rough weather, throwing up waves huge enough to swamp the largest boat, if not given due respect. So when in doubt let the fish go without—they'll be around for a feed the next day, so make sure you are.

It is the browns more than the rainbows that most often grace the bottom of our huge landing nets—especially in the streams, from which the latter usually make their escape to the sea. But in the dams the rainbows have settled down rather nicely, and have been taken up to 8 kg.

Rainbows were first introduced to Tasmanian waters in 1893, when a shipment of eggs from California was hatched and eventually released in Lake Leake. A few years later the Great Lake received them, and now almost every lake and dam in the state of Tasmania supports a good head of rainbow trout—or steelheads, as the Americans call them.

The grand-daddy of all trout was a brownie of over 17 kg captured from Scotland's Loch Awe in 1866, while the best from Tasmania is reputed to be that taken by Sir Robert Hamilton (then Governor of Tasmania) from the River Huon in 1887. His fish was around 13 kg but, as already mentioned, one of an estimated 14.5 kg came from Lake Cresent in 1973. It's anyone's guess which represents the record, or even how long such a record will remain a record. A dedicated few of the local fishermen swear that Lake Pedder is quite capable of producing a fish of above 15 kg; is there no end in sight?

We then have the brook trout, less widely distributed than its much larger relation. The brookie attains a weight of not much more than 2 kg, yet it's a real demon on the end of a line, and on a plate some say is the tastiest trout of all. Re-introduced from Canada in 1962-after previous attempts at acclimatisation had failed, the brook trout is now self-supporting in the Clarence Lagoon, but elsewhere is maintained by annual stocking in enclosed waters.

Within the Highlands of Tasmania conditions are absolutely perfect for the top-notch trout fisheries that abound there. More than 3000 lakes and lagoons are said to be in this region alone. Here the Great Lake and Arthurs Lake, plus the Echo, King William and the St Claire Lake occupy between them an unbelievably vast area, while the smaller waters like the Little Pine Lagoon and hundreds of similar lakes offer trout fishing of international repute—particularly during the months of December to March, when the hatches of mayfly bring the fish to the top. Mere words cannot describe the action then.

A number of waters have yet to be named, and are therefore absent on most maps of the region. Access to a great number is difficult too, even with a four-wheel-drive, although the Great Lake presents no such problems, a fact which makes it one of the more popular. And why not? It is certainly one of the best.

Launceston in the north is the main base for those who prefer to fish the rivers—and what rivers they are! Brumbys Creek is perhaps the finest of all, yet is a mere 15-km stretch of racing, surging water. Situated 25 km from Launceston, it richly deserves a visit because big browns and rainbows rise well to a fly during the mayfly hatches.

The St Patricks River is a delightful little stream, providing excellent sport on the fly, although the fish aren't particularly big. This and Brumbys Creek, along with the North and South Esks and their tributaries, such as the Isis, Elizabeth, Macquarie and Lake River, are patronised more than most by anglers, especially when the Red Spinner hatch gets underway. Brumbys Creek receives the waters of the Great Lake near Cressy to give it that extra bit of lustre.

In the south we have Lake Pedder, mightiest of all the lakes in the state. Right alongside Pedder is Lake Gordon, another huge sheet of water that makes the others look like mere duck ponds. Here in the south we discover fewer waters than up north, but there's still a great many of them. Much of the fishing is done in the streams: the Styx, Plenty, Russell, Shannon and Ouse. The Derwent River, dammed in parts, now forms pondages in which swim good fish. The Huon creeps into Pedder, as do many other streams, to help promote the fantastic fishing it offers.

But how does one discriminate between so many fine waters, let alone do them justice in print? They almost defy description in writing, yet for the majority this must suffice. For those who wish to venture to the places themselves, the magnificent lakes and streams in which the trout dwell, there are surprisingly well organised outlets for the hire of boats, as well as for cars and campervans that may be parked at any one of the service areas springing up for the benefit of the angler. Transport to and from the

While South Australia does not boast the trout fishing of other states, it is possible to catch a feed in the small streams within easy reach of Adelaide.

A Purrumbete rainbow.

A brace of fine callop. This warm-water species is widely distributed; it settles in the smallest of dams and offers some really grand sport on baits or spinners.

Carp such as these are abundant in the backwaters of the River Murray in South Australia.

Trout like these are commonplace up in the Snowy Mountains.

A nice yellow-belly is beaten to the net.

Redfin are distributed in many states, and are usually self-supporting. The stripes
and colour in the fins tend to fade with age.

A tiny redfin like this makes a first-class bait for really big redfin.

state across the water is also regular and reliable.

Indeed, arrangements can be made for a party to be picked up at the airport on arrival, if desired, with self-drive transport waiting and even a guide, if the best is to be made of the visit. And remember that as many hands make for lighter work, so also many anglers can make for lighter expenses all round.

## LAKES AND STREAMS

### Arthurs Lake

Arthurs Lake is a highly appreciated water found to the east of Great Lake. Many anglers prefer to fish here instead of the more publicised Lake Pedder. Classified as a brown trout water, it is open to angling from August to April. Originally Arthurs Lake consisted of two smaller natural lakes that were stocked at various intervals with browns and rainbows from as early as 1870. Atlantic salmon were released in one of the lakes in 1907, and Sebago salmon in 1911.

The Hydro-Electric Commission in 1964 erected a wall across the outlet at the Lake River, inducing the water level to rise until the two lakes became one in 1969. The growth-rate of the trout, which had always been acceptable, now took a sudden turn for the better, to produce an average weight of 2.5 kg. But, sadly, the changed character of the water created excellent new breeding conditions for the trout, which boosted the population and eventually resulted in a smaller-sized strain.

Angling afloat is a short-cut to the fish, but land-based fishermen are also in with a chance. Cowpaddock Bay, at the northern end of the dam, is the fly-fancier's territory, as is Pumphouse Bay, Hydro Bay and Morass Bay. Large hatches of mayfly emerge during the summer season and get the fish on the move, and it is at such times that the best catches are made. Among the favoured dry flies are March brown and Hardy's favourite.

Trolling is another proven method of taking good fish, and is in no way restricted to certain areas. Lures like the black and red Devon are suggested, although trout are more than likely to decide to take an entirely different type of lure when the occasion suits them, so don't hesitate to compromise. Spinning and live-baiting also produce results.

### Brumbys Creek

Acclaimed by some as the finest trout water in Tasmania, Brumbys Creek has a considerable reputation to live up to. Certainly it is a fantastic piece of water—easily one of the best—but to suggest it is the finest of all in a land where any one of a thousand could fit the description is simply asking for comments to the contrary. It is nevertheless a stream to be proud of, as those who have fished this swiftly moving river will no doubt readily agree. In January the angling is at its best, and the fly-fisher as contented as he is ever likely to be. Exactly what his pattern will consist of is decided largely by what insects the weather has hatched. The cocky spinner, dun, orange quill, black nymph and similar imitations will all catch fish when conditions are right. The nightstalker is advised to try a black muddler from dusk until dawn, when the biggest fish of all are on the prowl.

## Great Lake
With a shoreline of 150 kilometres, no wonder it's called the Great Lake. This is the largest of the central lakes, and is found at an altitude of more than 1000 metres. First stocked with brown trout in 1870, followed by rainbows in 1910, the water lived up to its expectations until the middle 1940s, when the sport began to falter. Many factors accounted for this, including an over-abundance of fish in relation to edible matter in the lake and also a spell of low rainfall, which called for a general increase in electric power. It is said that within a decade or two the rainbows for which the lake was noted had almost disappeared. And then began an operation to save the remainder. The Inland Fisheries Commission began to trap the thousands of brown trout headed for the spawning grounds in the Liawenee Canal, and to restock the lake heavily with rainbow fry. It took a few years to ascertain the results of this venture, but all concerned agree it has been an astounding success; the fishing has improved tremendously since then. The wattle grub, fished right on the bottom or inched patiently across it, has earned a reputation for tempting the fish during the night or day. Lure-fishing is also very popular, with red and black, green and gold, and black and gold spoons, flatfish, etc. Bait-fishing is prohibited in the areas of Little Lake, Canal Bay and Tods Corner, where only artificial lures may be used. Both trolling from a boat and spinning from a bank are successful on this water. And towards dusk the fly-fishers congregate in Tods Corner or where the Marlborough and Lake highways meet.

A beetle pattern of any kind is the recommended fly, along with Greenwells glory, ginger and black, Hackle's perfection, the black spinner, etc, depending on the weather. Wet fly imitations include the mallard, Watson's fancy and the butcher. Fishing is permitted on the Great Lake from November to June (except Canal Bay, which closes in April). Fishing is forbidden at all times whenever water flows into the lake.

## Little Pine Lagoon
One of the smaller Tasmanian lakes, Little Pine Lagoon is designated as a fly-only water, and is open during the brown trout season: early August to late April/early May. The Little Pine offers some of the most consistent sport found in the highland lakes, and is on the outer fringes of the Western Lakes belt. Trout from here average at around 1.5 kg, with the better fish weighing in at above 2.5 kg. It is susceptible to unpredictable changes in the weather, and the angler must keep a keen eye peeled for the insect hatches, being prepared to change flies accordingly. Prolific growths of weed in the lake help to create and maintain the aquatic insects on which the fish get big and fat. The most promising period to visit the Little Pine Lagoon is from November to the end of February.

## Lake Pedder
Along with Eucumbene Lake in New South Wales and Lake Argyle in the Kimberley of Western Australia, Lake Pedder is claimed to be the largest sheet of water in Australia. Each is enormous beyond words. On a map Lake Gordon appears to be almost as large as Pedder; however, the latter gets the limelight, and rightly so, judging by the giant trout it provides. To some, Pedder *is* Tasmania; whatever other waters exist there are of no concern to them. It has been written that every trout in Pedder is a mighty

one. Now wherever big fish are found, there must be smaller ones present; they're not born as monsters, after all. Yet in Pedder such logic doesn't seem to apply. If a fish is hooked then it's usually a big 'un. So whatever happens to the little fish? Nobody cares, of course, but it's an intriguing mystery, for there must be some tiny fish in the lake.

The lake was formed by the damming of the Serpentine River in 1972, and it didn't take the Pedder trout long to hit the headlines. They must be world-renowned by now, and will soon be attracting those anglers who go to New Zealand from all around the world. It's an untamed water, treating with scorn those who scoff at the danger signs when Pedder is in an angry mood. Yet at dusk it can be soothing, embracing with loving care those who wade chest-high in its shallows to tender a fly to the trout from dusk until the arrival of a chilly dawn. Often, the long, drawn-out vigil has been in vain—but on other occasions eruption after eruption on the water's surface are almost frightening, because Pedder trout don't simply rise for a fly, they create an upheaval of the dam to get at it—and why not? They're big enough to cause such a sensation. They appear as miniature submarines when finally drawn to the net after displaying the speed of a rocket and the mobility of a fox let loose in a chicken-run.

Lake Pedder forms part of the South-West National Park and is bounded on the north and east by conservation areas. The span of the lake covers 403 240 hectares, and that's a lot of water to search for a few fish! Local advice is a godsend in this case, as it is in most others, and the services of a guide really can work godlike miracles. Whatever advantages can be obtained before the great assault on those Pedder giants, should be acquired, balancing the chances of success a little more in our favour. Perhaps then we'll see our own grinning faces and catch peering back at us from our photograph in the magazine pages. Unless we're extremely unlucky our fish will be real beauts, because from Pedder the average catch is approximately 4.5 kg. Imagine that now. Doesn't that do something to the old adrenalin?

## Penstock Lagoon

A fly-only water, Penstock Lagoon is smaller than most and therefore not so much of a challenge in finding the fish, although a small lake in Tasmania might be considered a mighty big one elsewhere. Like all brown waters, the lagoon is open to fishing from August until the end of April, but the area known as Canal No. 2 (which carries water at times from Shannon Lagoon to Penstock) does not permit angling until November, which is when the rainbow season opens; it closes again at the beginning of April. Considered as one of the more picturesque lakes in the region, its waters lapping the large wattles and gums, the fish it supports are generally smaller than those found in the proud Pedder, averaging out at between 1.5–2 kg. But, of course, trout far bigger than this are taken from Penstock Lagoon each season.

## Lake St Clair

A beautiful name for an equally beautiful water, surrounded by snow-capped mountains. Fourteen km in length and 2 km wide, the water isn't a particularly big one. It is bigger by far than Penstock Lagoon, which is a mere 2 km long and 0.8 km wide, but still just a puddle compared to Lake

Pedder. Shaded by forests along its shores, we have a water well loved by the few who rise to the special challenge it offers. It's a deep sheet of water with little weed growth about the margins to coax the fish in, except where some shallows are located at the southern end of the lake. Here trout of up to 2 kg or more are often persuaded to meet the angler's net.

## Lake Sorell
Unlike Pedder, Gordon, and a few other large waters, Lake Sorell is a natural creation, with brown trout and rainbows that are completely self-supporting—they need the help of no man to propagate the species. Some anglers believe this to be the most rewarding water of all. It's a fine fishery whatever its position in terms of productivity, and presents some first-rate sport on either flies or trolled lures. Baits are not to be used. The fish are said to range from a kilogram to 3 kg—not the biggest to be found, but great fun to tangle with nevertheless.

## Other Waters
Among the other lakes waiting to be fully investigated is the myriad known as the Western Lakes. These include such waters as Lagoon Bay, Botsford, Ada and Ada Lagoon, Rocky Lagoon, Carter Lakes . . . there's simply no end to them. Those mentioned may be reached at various points along the Lake Augusta Road, and until recently weren't fished to any great degree—and for most of the time they are still virtually unfished. These are just a few of the waters located to the west of Great Lake, and are in the main brown trout waters, with fish up to 4.5 kg being taken quite regularly by the sprinkling of anglers that recognise the waters' potential.

Howes Lagoon Bay and Carter Lakes exist for the fly-fisher only, while on most of the others bait-fishing is condemned. Travel within the region is quite possible by conventional vehicles providing they don't stray from the regular tracks.

Other waters worthy of mention must follow in the wake of Lake Crescent, the trout therein being gifted with an incredible growth-rate. An inexhaustible supply of native galaxias accounts for this, so extra-large fish are by no means uncommon here. In fact, it was from this lake that the best trout from Tasmania was taken in 1973, one believed to have weighed 14.5 kg. In 1971 a brown of 12.3 kg was had, and in August the following year no fewer than four fish above 9.1 kg were caught, the best registering 12.3 kg. Each fell to a galaxias minnow fished on the bottom, which is the favoured method and bait for getting amongst the better fish.

The Lagoon of Islands Lake is unique in that islands in the shape of clumps of tea-tree suspended in the water make it different from other Tasmanian lakes. Created in the early 1960s by a wall built across a tributary of the Blackburn Creek, this water contains brown trout, having failed as a rainbow fishery some years ago. At the height of the hatch of large mayflies in early November, the nymphs crawl on to the tea-trees on the islands in the lake and end up in the water in their thousands, to bring the trout around. It leaves little to the imagination to visualise the sport had at that time, and from a power boat the dry-fly angler works around each island with a small March brown or a Hardie's favourite. Casting a natural bait to the fish will also account for some action, and generally either a worm or mudeye is on the hook.

67

Many of the lakes less isolated are well developed fisheries with reasonable roadways, launching ramps, and in some cases even camping areas. But to obtain a true picture of the scene there, it is suggested that those planning a visit contact Tasmanian Tourist Bureaus, where the officers really are helpful and willing to forward all the information necessary for a trip. The relevant addresses will be found at the back of this book, so use them to your advantage.

Some consideration should also be given for the weather, which is anything but agreeable for most of the time, and should therefore be fully assessed when packing the waterproofs and other clothing. A woolly jumper may be quite adequate for a day's fishing on a Victorian stream, but on the great lakes of Tasmania it will be no warmer than a cotton vest.

The most effective lures appear to be wobblers that have splashes of red, green or yellow; revolving-blade spinners coloured red or green with a gold base; brown Devon, green and gold spinners of most kinds and assorted flatfish. Fishcake lures are particularly killing on Lake Pedder. Wet flies include black and red matuka, green matuka, Watson's fancy, tadpole and yeti. Also useful are black or brown seals, fur nymphs and a small black beetle. Favoured dry flies are cockybondhu, red and black spinner mayfly, March brown or similar, and Greenwell's glory.

Baits on the lakes where they are permitted include worms, wattle grubs, grasshoppers and galaxia minnows, all of which can be obtained locally. A piece of scallop won't be ignored either. Frogs on the top at night are bound to succeed if fished in the shallows where the trout will expect to find them. It should be added, however, that tiger and copperhead snakes are common throughout the south-west, so it pays to be a little careful when hunting for frogs in territory that is also ideal for snakes.

## THE TASMANIAN FISHING YEAR

From Tasmania comes a month-by-month account of the situation likely to be found there, which will assist those contemplating a visit to select the most promising time in which to make their bid for a few trophy trout.

*August–September:* The rivers are often flooded during this period, creating near-perfect conditions for angling in the backwaters. Some of the lakes on a lower plain will fish reasonably well, i.e. Sorell, Crescent and Leake.

*October–November:* With the warmer weather come the hatches of flies in the lowland rivers and streams. The noted red spinner mayfly hatch is the most celebrated by the angler and fish. Tadpoles in the lower lakes will now coax the trout to the edge, making them an easier target on an imitation. The central highland lakes will shortly experience a similar activity.

*December–January:* Here we have the peak period of the angling scene in Tasmania. Each and every water will be producing large numbers of good fish. Huge hatches of mayfly and caddis moths send the fish into a frenzy of feeding as they rise to the surface to get their fill. Tadpole and dragonfly activity within the margins at this time adds to the overall attraction of being at the water's edge.

*February–March:* The lakes and streams in the highlands of Tasmania are now the wise angler's choice, for temperatures here will still be acceptable to the fish, while lower down the hot, dry weather may well affect the sport in all but the fastest of streams and the deepest of stillwaters. Beetles rather than flies now fill the air and alight on the water's surface, so a good imitation will be especially killing.

*April–May:* The trout fishing season is now sadly coming to an end. Insect falls are now spasmodic, and therefore so is the fishing. The subject of closures is reviewed each year, and tends to vary slightly. But if the season has been a good one, then huge trout by the score will have been lifted from the waters of Tasmania—but probably many more will have made good their escape.

## FISHING REGULATIONS

*Licence Fees:* (Annually) adult male, $15; adult female, $12; junior angler aged between ten and seventeen years, $1.50; approved pensioner, $5. Fourteen-day licence, $6.50; one-day licence, $3.50; replacement of lost licence, 50c. Children under ten are not required to have a licence.

*Open Season:* This is normally from the beginning of August to early May on most waters, with a slight variation in the case of rainbow trout. But since the close season may also vary on different waters it is advisable to check this matter out carefully before embarking on a visit. Many waters are closed at all times, and these should be noted with care. Other lakes and streams are reserved for fly-fishing only, and some restricted to artificial flies and lures, not permitting bait-fishing (Lake Pedder comes under this classification).

*Legal minimum sizes:* Brown trout, rainbow, brook trout: 220 mm. A bag limit of twelve trout is in force. Other regulations apply strictly to individual waters, and should therefore again be checked on before wetting a line. Such rules and regulations are enforced on our behalf to protect the future potential of our sport, so please obey them.

## BOAT-HIRE

As easily as the angler can rent a van so he can rent a boat. Aluminium craft of 4 m with 6-hp motors and trailers, plus all safety equipment for four persons can be hired from Rent-A-Boat, 147 Invermay Road, Launceston.

*Pedder Hire Boats* are found on the shore of Lake Pedder, where 4-m 'Islander' dinghies can be hired with all the usual safety gear for four persons, propelled by a 6-hp Johnson motor. Others of 2.4 m may be fitted with canopies and rod holders. Boats are either available on trailer or moored at the jetty below Lake Pedder Chalet. Runabouts of 5 m are also offered, with forward controls, canopy, screen and rod holders, and powered by two motors, 40–35–25 hp, and a 6-hp auxiliary, capable of carrying four passengers. Speed-boat licence essential; any state licence accepted. Contact Nigel and Elizabeth Heaven.

Also available at Pedder Hire Boats is the largest selection of trout lures in the south-west. Free service for freezing fish, ice, maps, fishing licences, up-to-the-minute information on fishing Lake Pedder, weigh-in centre. Guide and charter launch available with all gear if booked in advance. Open seven days a week.

The same place also offers fishermen's caravans on Lake Pedder. These are fully equipped for four persons. Linen can be hired at extra cost. Reduced rates with boat-hire. Contact for details about the Lake Pedder Chalet.

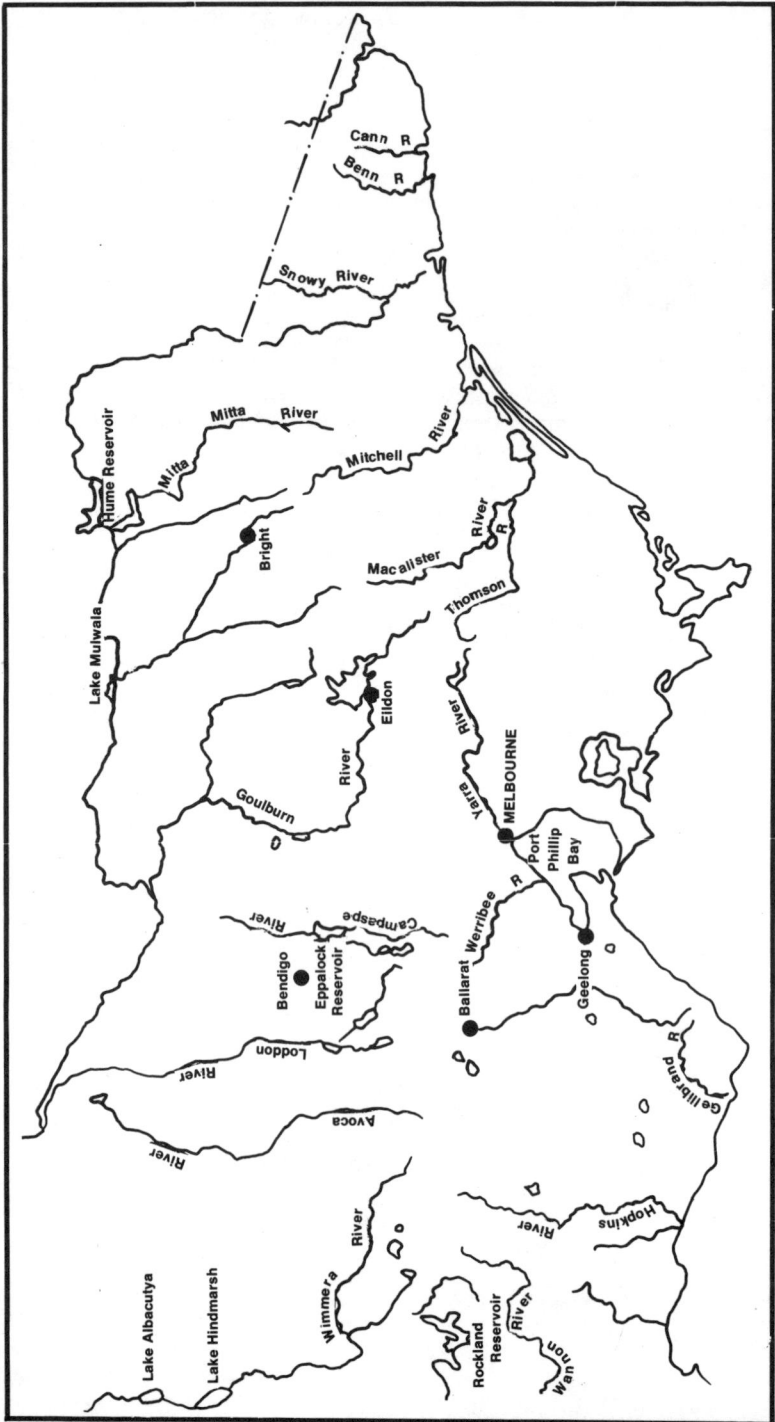

VICTORIA

Cann R
Benn R
Snowy River
Mitta River
Hume Reservoir
Mitta
Mitchell River
Bright
Macalister
River R
Thomson
Eildon
River
Goulburn
Yarra River
MELBOURNE
Port Phillip Bay
Campaspe River
Eppalock Reservoir
Bendigo
Werribee R
Ballarat
Geelong
Loddon River
Avoca
Gellibrand R
River
Hopkins River
Lake Albacutya
Lake Hindmarsh
Wimmera River
Rockland Reservoir
Wannon River
Lake Mulwala

# VICTORIA

Victoria, popularly known as the 'garden state', may be more aptly named the 'state of Aquarius' since it carries so much water—most of it fresh-water, supporting the species of fish life in which we as anglers have an avid interest.

From all points of the compass there's water—just a mere trickle in parts, where the creeks farewell the mother streams to journey on alone. Some have nothing but eels and tiny forage fish to boast of, while others have a few additional blackfish and puny trout that interest us not in the least. But a few contain surprisingly big fish for such mere whispers of water, the Myrtle Creek section of the Campaspe River drainage basin being one of them.

Then there are the streams, pretending to be fully-fledged rivers as they course their way proudly to journey's end. They're classified as rivers but are in reality small pretentious streams—yet some carry fish that are large enough to put the inhabitants of some proper rivers to shame. The Jamieson River, for example, is little more than a stream for most of its length, but produces exceptionally fine fish at times—bigger than those normally taken from some main river systems.

The deep, dawdling Goulburn River once presented to the angler fish of a size to be proud of, but now, alas, is losing its reputation fast. Some excellent fish are still supposed to be lying dormant at the bottom of snag-infested pools at the water's edge, flatly refusing to budge, but as an action-packed water the Goulburn must now rate poorly.

It is to the streams, rather than the big rivers, in fact, that most anglers turn when practising their art'because they, and not the rivers, lend themselves most vividly to our interpretation of what fishing is all about. The dry-fly angler is perhaps more aware of the transformation that takes place within us at the water's edge than any other; for the very nature of his calling demands his continued observation of the minute life forms created about him. His eyes must detect whatever insects are floating on the surface, if he hopes to match them with a fly; so is it surprising then that he is so much a part of that scene, blending in naturally as his fly settles delicately on the surface to leave a ripple there? I think not. And I have often regretted not having allowed this form of angling to be more important to me, for fly-fishing affords us the visions that we as anglers are most able to identify with.

Yet in this state of Aquarius, it is the presence of the bait-fisher or spinning enthusiast that coincides most often with the capture of the biggest fish, partly because these fish normally come from reservoirs and lakes too huge to be fished profitably by any but the most skilled fly-fisher, and partly because there are fewer of them in any case. But, generally, Victoria caters for all kinds of fishermen with its rivers and streams—and with its dams, that come in a variety of shapes and sizes.

It may be said that should all the waterways suddenly run dry, then the state would be riddled with the scars left behind. These scars would be noticeably more clustered in some areas than others, where thank God they're still very much filled with water and fish.

In the region of western Victoria, for example, there's a series of lakes, some of which are by their presence freaks of nature, having been created by a volcanic eruption long before the cave dwellers fashioned the first fish hook out of bone or whatever to give birth to a sport that perhaps still hasn't reached its pinnacle. A few of these waters lack the chemical make-up needed to support fish of any kind. But the remainder include first-rate fisheries, containing some exceptionally fine fish.

Camperdown is the home-ground of Lake Bullen Merri and the celebrated Lake Purrumbete which is world renowned for the magnificent rainbow trout that have come from its depths—fish of over 9 kg. Both lakes also contain quinnat salmon, to offer the kind of fishing unique to this land.

Ballarat can boast of Burrumbeet, Wendouree and Learmonth lakes, to mention but a few of the many concentrated within the area that was once noted more for its gold than its fishing potential. Although some waters are omitted from this book because they lack the necessary rating as a fishery, that isn't to say that they're not worth visits if their performance proves satisfactory. It depends on what each individual expects from his efforts.

In the Eildon area there's virtually a spider's web of rivers and streams, most of which are related to the enormous reservoir known as Eildon Lake, that would leave the biggest and deepest scar of all should it suddenly run dry, to expose the sad remains of the old town that lies on the bottom, rotting away.

Then there's the moat-like Murray, acting as a natural border to other states. The River Murray is Australia's longest river, and has for the purpose here been listed in the 'Murray District' section of the New South Wales chapter, since the Victorian Inland Fishing Licence doesn't cover it (this is the case of a few other waters fondly thought of as Victorian, yet in fact they come under the jurisdiction of other states).

The cool mountain streams of Bright and the surrounding areas may perhaps be the most inviting of all. Here the fly-fisher can live out his fantasies to the hilt as he searches for the trout in streams that are, to him, created for no other purpose on earth.

We also have the Yarra, Melbourne's very own water. The fish it harbours are grossly underestimated, both in quantities and size. Big trout swim in the Yarra in reaches surprisingly close to the city. And not so long ago a nice Murray cod fell to the lure of an angler fishing from a boat anchored almost in Bourke Street. There are at the moment plans to clean up the Yarra, which may in time bring about the credit it so richly deserves, rather than the notoriety it lives under now.

The following pages list only a fraction of the number of waters available to those fishing in Victoria. To cover them all would in itself warrant a volume in its own right. However, most major and a few more minor waters have been dealt with. Any further queries may be sought from the Fisheries and Wildlife Division of Victoria.

## BRIGHT DISTRICT

The tiny alpine town of Bright is almost lost in a shroud of mist as it nestles amidst the towering peaks of the mountainous country that is Victoria's answer to the Snowy Mountains region of New South Wales. The higher plateaus of both districts are carpeted in snow for the best part of winter, creating the kind of breathtaking beauty normally to be found only on Christmas cards from areas beyond them. Indeed, so fairyland-like is the scenery at one particular point that no other name could describe it than Mount Beauty.

The similarities between the mountainous regions of both states are many, which is to be expected since both form part of the Great Dividing Range. And each is blessed with some magnificent trout fishing in the rivers and lakes that are, by the nature of their topographical setting, ideally suited to a species that much prefers the clearer, purer, and ice-cold waters of the high country.

The township of Bright, which is a pleasant 312-kilometre drive from Melbourne, taking you right through Ned Kelly country, acts as a natural base for those wishing to fish the many turbulent rivers and picturesque dams within reasonable distance of it. The town and adjacent villages are extremely well served with motels, hotels, caravan parks and cabins. The entire area is of course a tourist resort during certain times of the year, when city folk in their thousands come along to play on the snow, but that's no deterrent to the angler who, even at the height of the season, finds he seldom has to share the water with anyone.

He should choose wisely the ideal time to make his bid, if only to escape the attention of too many redfin, that amount to plague conditions during the months of summer, especially on the main Ovens River at Bright; and there's no way to stop them highjacking baits intended for the more acceptable trout—and that goes for most kinds of spinners! The redfin here stop at nothing to outwit the trout-seeker, who must in the end turn to his dry-fly gear. I suffered at the expense of these striped tormentors for the best part of a week because even at night they were there, haunting me with their continued presence while knocking-off all the bait. A slimy slug beat them in the end, while the trout went for this unlikely offering in a big way. I also managed to hook and land one large platypus here, that took a tiny frog fished on the bottom. However, overall the rivers, streams and dams are the domain of the fly-fishing fanatics.

## RIVERS AND LAKES

### Buckland River
Containing rainbow and brown trout, with the latter being more numerous, this water produces good results throughout most of the year. The average size of each fish taken isn't perhaps as large as those found in the Buffalo, for example, but they certainly let the angler know they're on the end of his line. Deep pools running over the gravelly bottom will host most of the better fish, and these may reach a weight of 3 kg. A drifted worm or grub is suggested as a means to tempt them during the early part of the day, and a dry fly such as a butcher or black ant may be tried as the sun sets.

### Buffalo Lake
Situated near Dandongadale, about 25 km from Bright, the lake covers an area of 340 hectares. Brown trout frequent the water in large numbers, and likewise the rainbows that attain a smaller size. Redfin, crucian carp and Macquarie perch also abound here in shoals big enough to offer quite a lot of sport in a variety of different techniques, the most popular being fly-fishing and spinning. From the lake the trout head for the Buffalo River in order to spawn.

### Buffalo River

Above the lake the river travels through heavily timbered terrain, then on past the tobacco fields, so much a feature of the area and amounting to quite an industry. Above the lake, rainbows are more abundant than browns, although below the dam the latter revert to their normal position by becoming the most prominent species. The other lake fish dwell in the river too, making it more interesting than most. The banks are more able to accommodate the angler downstream, where fly-fishing is considered the most killing. But a frog fished on top of the deep silent pools at night will bring up from the depths the better fish. Most waters within the vicinity of Bright lend themselves most readily to this form of fishing when the frogs are croaking near the water's edge, but it's then more difficult to catch some for baits. Seek them out in the daytime instead by concentrating on the kind of places where a snake might hide out, praying all the while that one isn't.

### Catani Lake

This is a small sheet of water found in the Mount Buffalo National Park, where the high altitude causes low temperatures in winter that fall to below freezing point. It is then that the rods leave the water and the ice-skates appear, for the lake freezes completely, encouraging a great deal of activity on its surface then. But beneath the ice are the fish, mostly brown trout, that are restricted somewhat in size. A 2-kg fish would be the best to expect from here, but on such a little lake they should be easier to find. About 20 km west of Bright, the lake is well worth a visit, because it's set in beautiful surroundings affording the angler with a camera some not-to-be-missed shots.

### Catherine River

Found at Mount Cobbler, the river is a fair distance from Bright, but offers some excellent fishing to the fly, spinner and bait enthusiast, but from November to April the fly-fisher will fair best. Like most others listed, the river runs through mountainous forested country, and over a clean, gravelly bed, where with the aid of polaroid spectacles the fish can often be seen lying on the bottom from which nothing at all will tempt them if the weather's too warm. The water is reached by walking along a track at the junction of the Buffalo River. It contains the usual rainbow and brown trout.

### Ovens River

Rising on the Bogong High Plains, above Bright, the Ovens River is fed by the small streams making their way down the slopes of Mount Buffalo. The Ovens and Buffalo rivers meet below Myrtleford, then journey on to the King River above Wangaratta, before continuing to Corowa, and the mighty Murray River.

The Ovens is the most popular stream around Bright, and the fly-fishermen catch the biggest bags of fish, lest they be redfin, in which case a baited hook will win hands-down. And the same can be said of the blackfish that appear in fair numbers here, to serve the angler's palate at least, although their sporting rating must be marked down as nil. Some excellent spinning for redfin and trout will add to the catch when the fish aren't rising to the top, and a celta, wobbler, or Devon minnow have proved their worth here. Although most lures and fly patterns may be easily obtained in the township of Bright, gathering together a supply of bait is not so readily dealt with, especially during the summer months, when the ground becomes rock-hard, and refuses to respond to spade or garden fork. It is advisable therefore to collect the bait beforehand, and don't let the redfin get at it.

## TOURIST ATTRACTION—MOUNT BUFFALO NATIONAL PARK

This is situated in the mountains in north-east Victoria, 320 kilometres from Melbourne. It is a tourist venue in winter, where a chair lift is in operation. Snow sports include skating on the surface of Lake Catani after a heavy freeze. Fishing and boating take place on the lake during summer. Bushwalking, horse riding and tennis are all part of the summer scene. Ideal for photography, with magnificent alpine scenery, high views from the plateau, and winter snow. Just 8 km from Bright, the park is well worth a visit, being a part of the great panoramic beauty that is so typical of the area. Eucalypt forests are found at a lower level and on the higher plains alpine flora flourishes to add its silent splendour to the scene. The Horn, at 1720 metres is the highest point in the park. A camping and caravan park is open from November to May, but no power is available. No pets are permitted but sites can be booked in advance for holiday periods by phoning the park ranger.

# EILDON LAKE DISTRICT

Approximately 139 kilometres from Melbourne lies Eildon Lake and its attendant rivers and streams, offering the angler some first-rate trout fishing. The lake itself is enormous, with a surface area of 13 840 hectares and a shoreline of 515 kilometres. The maximum depth is 76 metres.

Formerly regarded as one of the finest trout waters in the country, its fishing has deteriorated quite considerably, due mainly to the wall of the weir being raised to lift the level of the lake. This in turn flooded the weed beds in the shallows and the favoured fishing spots adjacent to them, leaving steep banks that in many parts makes access to the lake difficult.

Much of the margin fishing is now defunct because the depth of the water does not allow the rays of the sun to penetrate to the bottom where they're needed to encourage the growth of plant life, necessary to act as host to the various forms of insect life that coax the trout close into the edge.

However, there's still some great fishing to be had in parts—around the weir arms, for example, where trolling appears to be the most accepted method. A good selection of lures is recommended to enable the angler to experiment a little with each until some fish are encountered. Much will depend on the clarity of the water, the season, and whatever living creatures are there for the fish to feast on.

Bait-fishing and spinning are practised mainly in the inlets and bays, where good trout, redfin, and the occasional Murray cod, callop, or Macquarie perch are sought, though the presence of these Murray species in worthwhile numbers must be somewhat doubtful these days.

## EILDON LAKE WATERS

### Bonnie Doon

One hundred and seventy-seven kilometres from Melbourne (map ref. I), Bonnie Doon is undoubtedly the most popular of the bays. Redfin predominate here, and are to be taken on worms, yabbies, small spinners and bait-fish. Trout-fishing comes into its own when the level of the lake drops to expose the bordering grasslands, for as the water rises again the trout move in to feed. Fair numbers of the species may also be had at times in the area above the Mansfield Road. At night some good trout are to be taken close to the edge. A few suggested fly patterns to try in the area are red and black matuka, the green and black woolly worm, the stick caddis nymph on a size 13 hook and the black beetle wet pattern with long tail to represent a tadpole. The ever popular cockybondhu also warrants a try. A camping area and boat ramp is to be found near Kennedy Point, reached by the Maintongoon Road. A caravan park also exists within the area, and the township of Bonnie Doon is close to the lake.

### Eildon Township

This makes a good base for fishing the lake and pondage (map ref. 2). There's some respectable trout to be found when trolling the less frequented bays of the lake proper; but it should be remembered that this area is very much a tourist attraction, which doesn't help the fishing much unless one concentrates on the pondage. The township boasts a cinema, sportsground, shops, houses, flats and a motel.

### The Pondage

Nearby, the pondage is of more interest to the angler after a few big trout—and there are plenty that grow to an incredible size in this water. Each year more are added from the surplus stock of fish at the Snobs Creek Hatchery. It's not particularly easy fishing (what kind is?) and the majority who try for the trout tend to rely most often on a bubble float that's cast well out from the bank with a worm or mudeye just a metre or two below it.

Others spin with a variety of spoons and lures, while a few prefer to present their bait on the bottom fished on a leadless line. Casting out a bait, allowing it to sink and then retrieving it again erratically, is almost guaranteed to succeed. Night-fishing is also popular here, and many fine fish are tempted on baits fished on the bottom; those suspended nearer the surface or actually fished on it, such as a cricket or frog. Early morning, evening, or throughout the night is the best time to be at the waterside, and the black matuka fished slowly on the fly-gear may well afford the angler manipulating it some exciting, breathtaking moments.

A caravan park is situated on the left of the upper pondage lake and a picnic area is to be found on the right. Although no boats are allowed on the pondage, fishing is permitted throughout the year.

### Gough Bay

This is reached from Piries, 7 km away on the Delegate River Road, also offers some decent trout angling, and is credited with still producing the odd Murray cod near the mouth of the Howqua River.

**Snobs Creek**

Snobs Creek (map ref. 4) is not a fishery but a hatchery, and therefore of considerable interest to the visiting angler. Here is where the future trout and quinnat salmon are hatched and later released in the waters of Victoria. Between 10 a.m. and 4 p.m. daily visitors may see all aspects of the research and experimentation taking place at the fishery research centre and hatchery. A small entrance fee is charged, which is well worth paying for the pleasure of glimpsing some mighty great trout in the holding ponds. The hatchery is situated just 5 km from Eildon Weir which, incidentally, holds more water than Sydney Harbour.

**Taylor Bay**

Taylor Bay (map ref. 5), 4 km north-west of the Eildon township, is another favourite venue, mainly for the redfin fishing close in amongst the submerged trees in the area. Some exceptionally big perch are to be had by those capable of keeping them away from the snags. Some excellent trout can also be expected on spoons that are trolled deeply.

## THE TROUT STREAMS

Many trout streams flow in to Eildon Lake at various points, the most important from an angling point of view being those listed below. Each may be influenced by the level of the lake. But the weir at the head of the pondage lakes creates a set of conditions relating to the Goulburn River that defy understanding. At the height of summer the angler may meet a river that is running swift and swollen, while in the grip of winter, when most other streams are filled to the brim, the Goulburn may appear as placid as a mill pond.

Such conditions are not for the novice to combat. Yet each and every fish he does manage to deceive into taking a bait must account for a feather in his cap. The most often used baits in the district of Eildon are earthworms or Jap clams, although pieces of scallop, grubs, slugs, grasshoppers and crickets should all be given a fair go when available.

Frogs fished on the top at night will account for any number of good trout, although frogs as bait are now banned in most states, but not yet in Victoria. There's a strong possibility however that by the time this appears in print that may well be the case, so those intending to give frogging a go are well advised to check on this matter further.

Each stream is reassessed at least every year for stocking, and enough trout are maintained in them to keep us all contented. Yet despite the unceasing dedication of the Fisheries and Wildlife officers concerned, there can be no denying that the trout fishing in this area is going steadily downhill.

Many anglers attribute this to the abolition of the close season in Victoria, and the fact that fish may now be retained whatever their size. Perhaps they are right, but by the time that is proved it may well be too late to do much about it. But whatever the cause, the fishing is worsening in parts that a decade ago could be relied upon fully to give us some sport.

Nowadays the angler is hard-pressed to obtain the acceptable bag of fish that once was taken for granted. Yet those familiar with the streams still manage to catch their fair share, although they find they're working harder at it. Some rely more heavily on a well activated spinner that allows them to cover more water, while the bait-fisher, too, is more mobile, trying this hole and that until a couple of fish are netted, and then moving along to the next, hoping to repeat the performance. But it's hard plodding all the way, with little or nothing to show at the end of it. It is to be hoped that those responsible will achieve something better before our streams turn into lifeless drains.

## MURRAY RIVER AND VALLEY TOWNSHIPS

For all Victorian waters relating to the Murray River, see the 'Murray District' section of New South Wales.

### Acheron River

A delightful little stream that presents the ideal setting for dry-fly-fishing. Not too wide for most of its length, the Acheron is clear enough in parts to enable the beginner to get some practice in with his fly-stick. Most of the trout are tiny, unfortunately, but great little scrappers nonetheless. They're also to be had on floating hoppers or crickets. A bait dropped in the calmer pools on a sinkerless line will undoubtedly also encourage some fish to react. Perhaps a small lively worm or Jap clam is best, and a tiny split-shot may be added to the finest of lines to get the bait down in the faster runs. A few suggested fly patterns are black and brown ants, royal coachman, butcher, and Wickham's fancy.

A quaint little wooden bridge once crossed the river at Glendale Lane, but now a concrete one has replaced it, ruining the scene completely. Some interesting nymph fishing can be had in the faster water between Buxton and Taggerty, and a worm drifted down on a free line is also worth a try.

### Big River

Mostly bait-fishing is to be found here, although certain spots do lend themselves more to spinning and fly-fishing. From the Eildon-Jamieson Road upstream, some average sport may be experienced with either method. The upper reaches near Stockmans Reward consist mainly of short narrow passages and deep pools; useful for probing with a bait and practising the ancient art of dapping an insect on the surface of the water where other insects of all kinds obviously drop from the tree branches overhead. Small wet flies in the larger pools may drum up a bit of action, but generally this is the bait-fisher's territory.

### Delatite River

Once renowned for the massive Murray cod in the Delatite Arm, this water is now a mere shadow of its former self. These days the catch is more likely to be a redfin than anything else. Rising to the north-east of Mount Buller, the Delatite shoots through to Mirrimbah, then on to Merrijig, Delatite and finally Eildon Lake. In between are variations to the character of the banks, overgrown in parts to such an extent that even bait-fishing is doubtful, while further along one can cast a fly with little chance of a hang-up. When the waters of Lake Eildon rise in spring to affect the level of the river, some nice trout from the lake occasionally venture into the Delatite to accept wet and dry flies. It is said that the standard of fishing here depends much on the winter just passed, because if rain falls heavily the fish enter the river. If not? Well, there are plenty more rivers around!

## Goulburn River

Probably one of the most popular streams in the area, though God knows why! The fishing here appears to have deteriorated at a faster rate than any other. There's still some fish to be taken—good fish, but they're uncannily cautious about taking a fly, bait or spinner. Indeed, their survival instinct is greater than I have ever encountered, which in a nutshell certainly means an unpredictable fishery. Yet still we try to beat them, knowing full well that every one we do deceive is worthy of a dozen elsewhere. The water from the pondage pools at Eildon, down through Thornton, Alexandra and on to Ghin-Ghin, represents a great variation to suit most techniques. Shallow streamy runs converge with deeper water sweeping into the banks to carry all manner of edible matter to the fish lying there. A succulent worm or grub lightly hooked in the head will on occasion call their bluff, or a fidgety spinner may be called upon to tempt them out of their paralytic stupor, but all too often nothing will do! Then, quite unexpectedly, they decide to feed, and that's when some good catches are made, without us doing a damned thing that's different! Whatever the problem, perhaps it will right itself in time. If the angler's lucky he may glimpse a platypus in the water here, or even see an early morning fox—but there's no need for luck to trip over a snake; in the summer the tigers are everywhere!

The upper reaches of the Goulburn, above Eildon Lake, tend to fish a lot better, although the trout are generally smaller than those below it. The banks are less obstructed and therefore more suitable for those who wish to wave a fly wand. This pursuit accounts for many fish at times, using Greenwell's glory, red tag, whirling dun, black and brown ants and the coachman, all in the smaller pattern.

## Howqua River

Some excellent fly fishing is to be enjoyed in the upper reaches of the Howqua, where clear, shallow water demands the use of the finest leaders that are rarely heavier than 4X. Favoured flies to be worked here, where some insist the best dry-fly-fishing in Victoria is to be had, are Greenwell's glory, small black and red matuka, the black beetle and similar flies. Not a place for clumsy bait-fishing gear, although a worm trickled down from a distance on an ultra-fine line will not go unnoticed. A grasshopper or mudeye floated on the fly rod is also killing at times.

The Howqua Inlet is also worth a visit, but difficult to fish from the bank when the water in the lake is low, because vast areas of thick mud lie between the angler and the fish. When conditions are right, however, to coincide with the appearance of stick caddis, tadpoles and the like, the fly-fisher is again in his element, using lures to represent the real thing. Some good spinning and trolling is also in the offing.

## Jamieson River

This is a picturesque stream that's always a delight to fish, whether with the fly, spoon or bait; although if you wish to succeed with bait here, you are advised to reduce the strength of the line and the size of the hooks and baits. Certainly a line of 2 kg is the maximum strength, and a line fifty per cent lighter in the right hands is quite sufficient. A single split-shot is adequate enough to act as the sinker but, better still, leave the line uncluttered of lead altogether, and allow the bait to act in a natural fashion, be it a worm, a grub of some kind, or even a most peculiar creepy-crawly picked up on the bank. The Jamieson is nevertheless the fly fancier's field of action, and during the summer months there's little to beat a well-tied grasshopper imitation. Other patterns include the small Wickham's fancy, red tag, cockybondhu, and Greenwell's glory. Two wet flies to try are a red and black matuka, and black beetle. Within the area of Gourleys Bridge in the lower reaches some reasonable bottom fishing can be expected when using worms, mussels, Jap clams or grubs for bait. Trolling or spinning may also pay dividends here.

### Rubicon River
The Rubicon River, being the last of those most noted in the area, is yet another more suited to fly-fishing. It is capable of producing only small trout mainly, although the better one does show occasionally to take everyone by surprise. A well patronised water during the spring and summer months, especially downstream towards the Thornton township, the Rubicon is nonetheless worthy of a trip or two, if only to perfect our striking at the little demons there, and to practise our cast. Most of the flies used successfully on other streams in the area will probably suffice on this tiny stream, but be sure to keep them small and the leader they're tied to as light as possible.

Other lesser streams exist within the region of Eildon Lake, and there are more further afield, most with their very own characteristics. It should be appreciated, however, that while the trout are incredibly small in comparison to those taken from some of the more famous waters, they're in no way inferior to them. Indeed, in extreme cases a fish of a kilo is equal to a 5 kg catch from the Eucumbene, and often surpasses it in terms of effort, skill, and dedication in learning of its whereabouts and then tempting it to the hook. So the angler should never feel dejected if the best he can manage on some of these streams is only small. It may well be the best fish in that particular water.

### OTHER VICTORIAN WATERS
### Barwon River
More widely renowned for the estuary fishing it produces, the Barwon River has nevertheless some good brown trout above the tidal reaches that are often overlooked by those with mulloway fever. Redfin, carp, numerous eels and the odd Macquarie perch are there too, probably begging for a bit of attention. Indeed, some of the best redfin fishing is to be had right within the city of Geelong. Baits should fish better on the bottom for all species, but local advice is always to be sought and adhered to whenever facing the dubious task of finding the fish in foreign territory. Accommodation of most kinds will be available in Geelong, as will supplies, including fishing gear and bait. If the trout are not biting then by all means join the mulloway madness; that is well justified during some years.

## Bemm River

Bemm River is another that's more suited to the estuarial fisherman than his freshwater counterpart, and is linked with the Mallacoota drainage system. Bream are the most prized species here, taken from the estuary in vast numbers at times. But big brown trout are also to be had by those with the patience to seek them out. They'll probably rely mostly on a good mouthful when deciding to feed, so a small bait-fish is well worth a try. Often, though, it's more difficult to catch the bait than the trout! Being nearer the mouth of the river may account for problems rarely met on more usual trout streams, so perhaps it's wiser to concentrate on those instead. The area is well served with caravan parks.

## Bolac Lake

Redfin are the predominant species here, and can be taken up to nearly a kilo in weight, although the average fish caught would be much smaller. It is imperative when wishing to dodge the weenies that large baits be used on hooks big enough to contain them securely, otherwise the angler will soon tire of reeling in one little perch after another.

A small live fish kept just off the bottom will entice the better fish while keeping their smaller brethren at bay. Indeed, even the tiniest of redfin will tempt his big brother, and it takes a lot of beating for big redfin especially. A small sinker stopped about a metre from the bait will allow it to wander at will around the bottom, where it will be more noticeable.

Fish baits may also be employed to catch some of the eels on the bottom of this lake, which probably grow to a couple of kilos at least; but night is the best time by far to sort the eels out, for they'll leave their dens among the rocks on the bottom then, and hunt in earnest for a fulfilling meal. Any dead fish will be to their liking, and should be fished on a wire trace. Worms will also attract them, of course, but as in the case of the redfin, a small fish on the end of the line will account for the biggest of all.

European carp and tench are also present in Bolac Lake, and rainbow trout are added at regular intervals. The water is shallow and generally quite discoloured, so baits with plenty of aroma must be the most killing here. Spinning lures that are bright enough to compensate for the density of the water and which also vibrate nicely will undoubtedly receive attention from the redfin and trout, and may be used in certain areas from a boat. The lake is situated close to the town bearing the same name.

## Lake Bullen Merri

Lake Bullen Merri is strictly the venue of those seeking quinnat salmon, that fish being the only species released in the lake of late. A few exceptionally large brown trout are said to roam near the bottom, feeding almost exclusively on the minnows that can be taken from the shallows in a trap.

It's the huge quinnat salmon, however, that are sought, fish of up to 12 kg that still remain from the 20 000 yearling fish liberated in 1978. Such fish have recently been found dead around the margins of the lake—proof enough of their existence—and there's never a lack of anglers out on the water tooled up to the hilt to do battle with these giants, although more recent results have been disappointing.

It is assumed that, like the trout, the best salmon have developed a taste for the minnows that are there for easy picking. Nevertheless, enough good fish are still to be had on lures and baits to warrant more than a single visit, especially when there's the possibility of a real big 'un putting in an appearance; just one of those is reward enough for any number of trips . . .

Here, perhaps more so than nearby Purrumbete Lake (that also contains monster quinnat), baits more commonly used in the bays are lowered deeply to entice a species that will accept most saltwater baits as readily as those associated with freshwater. Whitebaits and pilchards are very much in evidence on Bullen Merri, and don't necessarily have to be fished from the limited confines of a boat! Local anglers with more experience of the water will occasionally sneak out at night to fish either a whitebait or pilchard from the bank—and they wouldn't go to that trouble for nothing . . .

Lake Bullen Merri is an exposed and rather featureless sheet of water, with little protection around its shoreline, which covers 8.7 km. It's 2.62 km in length and 2.56 km wide, with a maximum depth in the centre of 66 m. The average depth is 39 m.

A boat ramp is available near the picnic area, and a caravan park exists within close proximity to the water. All angling techniques pertaining to the quinnat salmon in Lake Purrumbete are applicable also to Bullen Merri, and many anglers alternate their fishing on a daily or weekly basis between both lakes.

Like Purrumbete, this water is also subjected to closure according to the stocking programme in force at the time, so the appropriate authorities should be consulted before wetting a line.

A bag limit of 5 salmon per day is allowed, which may create all kinds of problems if each should happen to be a big 'un, not the least being the task of getting them all home! At the present time the normal amateur fishing licence to cover the inland waterways of Victoria also covers angling for quinnat salmon, although it is envisaged that at some time in the future a separate licence will be necessary to fish the waters they inhabit.

### Lake Burrumbeet
Situated at Ballarat, Lake Burrumbeet is a favourite piece of water of the locals especially, who revel in the bags of medium-sized rainbow trout that are to be had at times, although larger specimens do exist in the lake but are a bit more difficult to catch, though the angler should never stop trying for them. Enormous redfin of up to 2 kg may also be had by those experienced in relation to the better fish.

Almost anyone can catch smaller redfin when they are feeding in earnest, even the novice in our midst, but bigger redfin are a different kettle of fish altogether, if you'll excuse the pun, because monster redfin are almost fanatical in their sensitivity to even the finest of lines and the slightest of drags. Big redfin are also more likely to be had on a bigger bait, such as a large, wriggly worm or a bait-fish big enough to arouse its interest.

Carp, tench and eels also inhabit the water, which is quite shallow in comparison to other lakes in this part of the state and has a sandy bottom. Anglers fishing from the banks will find plenty of 'elbow room' in which to enjoy their sport. Prone to be whipped up by the wind at times, the lake does perhaps lure a few too many to fish it during the summer months, but it's quite a big sheet of water capable of catering for all manner of fishermen with their different techniques.

It fishes best in the early months of the season and suggested baits are worms, galaxias minnows, or gudgeon for the trout, eels and redfin, or bread dough or worms for the carp and tench. Some excellent eels may be had by those who fish after dark.

Celta and Flopy lures and hogback fly spoons may also be worked either from a boat or the bank to good effect on the redfin and trout, but line strengths should be kept to the absolute minimum.

## Cairn Curran Reservoir

This is an enormous expanse of water covering an area of 1918 hectares. Located at Newstead, Cairn Curran Reservoir is basically a deep water, with extensive shallows around the margins at the northern end to allow for the prolific growth of plant life there. This in turn encourages all manner of other minute living creatures to breed and feed within the weed beds, to add to the diet of the fish therein.

Decent-sized brown trout averaging out at a kilo in weight and perhaps advancing towards 3 kg produces the best fishing in the dam, particularly during winter and spring, when larger than normal baits should account for the best fish. Huge slimy slugs, scrubworms or bait-fish are suggested, fished on or near the bottom, while a lively frog on the top at night is bound to tempt a few fish—but keep them nearer the bank where the trout will be searching for them.

During March and April, fly-fishing and spinning is advised; the suggested lures being silver wobbler, Flopy, hogback spoon, celta, Devon minnow, etc—or whatever has proved its worth in the past, because choice of spinners will always be a personal thing. The flies most likely to bring some success are the black ant, red and black matuka, butcher, and the brown nymph.

Redfin, crucian carp and a few rainbow trout are also present in the water, and when in season the mudeye is claimed to be exceptionally killing. The redfin feed best during late summer and early autumn. A boat ramp and camping ground is found at the northern end of the lake, with all the normal facilities. An increase in flow from the Loddon River improves the fishing throughout the dam, which is stocked only occasionally with trout, but still worth the effort of getting amongst them.

## Coliban River

Brown trout, blackfish and redfin are to be encountered upstream from the Upper Coliban Reservoir, while in the small stretch between this and the Lauriston Reservoir rainbow trout are also to be had. A tiny narrow stream finding its way through grazing country, the Coliban is nevertheless well respected for the fishing it offers. Trout of above 2 kg can be taken during the spawning run from the Upper Coliban Reservoir to add flavour to the sporting potential of this lightly fished water. From Malmsbury Reservoir to Eppaloch Lake, the above species are joined by tench and crucian carp. The best fishing of all is said to be experienced just below Malmsbury Reservoir. Suggested tactics: small baits on ultra-fine lines. Good fly-fishing is to be had at times on the smaller variety of dry flies. The reservoirs mentioned above were once well worth the attention of the fly-fisher, but their potential is now considered by some to be wanting badly.

### Dock Lake
Not a particularly well known water, Dock Lake is sited near Horsham. Reasonably flat land surrounds the water to allow for the angler who prefers to fish from the bank, but boats are permitted. Big redfin and even bigger rainbow trout are to be lured from this not-so-large water that is stocked on a regular basis with trout that may grow to possibly 3 kg. Clear water is indicated as the best for trout fishing. The usual baits and lures should catch fish.

### Eppalock Lake
At 3200 hectares this lake is a huge one, with a sandy, rocky bottom. The shoreline is surrounded by forest in parts, but is clear enough in others to allow the angler to fish with ease from the bank. Some hefty brown trout live here, along with some equally hefty redfin, to compete for the baits and lures used to tempt them off the bottom. Tench, crucian carp and the occasional rainbow trout are also to be met, although sadly this water is no longer stocked regularly with any species. A caravan park, adjoining the huge weir wall, advertises (apart from the usual features) a mini-bike track and tennis court. There are also two other caravan parks on the lake.

### Fyans Lake
Reputed to have some monster rainbows of above 4 kg swimming in its depths, Fyans Lake is obviously an underrated water. Located near Halls Gap, this fishery produces an average size of a kilo for rainbow trout and very nearly 3 kg for browns, which is a terrific average for any water! Good redfin also abound here, but receive little consideration when so many fine trout are there for the catching. The best fish will invariably fall to the bigger baits—perhaps a live bait-fish near the bottom or a frog on the top—and will undoubtedly be far more active after dark. The fish are normally to be found in excellent condition, and therefore absolutely full of fight. This lake is regularly stocked with rainbow trout, and a camping ground exists on the eastern shore.

### Gellibrand River
Situated near the town that bears its name, the Gellibrand River is, despite the reputation it enjoys as a trout water, more geared to the estuary fisherman in the lower reaches, where Australian salmon, mullet, bream and estuary perch are taken. There are at present plans afoot to dam the river, much to the anger of the residents of the town of Gellibrand which will be flooded should the plans go ahead. Just what will happen to the fishing then is anyone's guess. There is no access for vehicles to the upper reaches, but they contain nothing but blackfish anyway. But at Princetown the angler can launch his boat or fish from the bank. Suggested baits are minnow, whitebait, small live fish and spew worms. Often stocked with brown trout.

## Glenmaggie Reservoir

A most popular water for all seasons, the township of Glenmaggie gives its name to the reservoir nearby. The water carries predominantly brown trout that attain at best 2 kg. A few rainbow trout, eels and crucian carp add to the interest of fishing here. Good sport is to be obtained from the banks as well as the boats, for this is generally a deep water dam, with few shallow areas for weed beds to grow. Fishing is claimed to be best during the autumn and spring, but some sport should be had at the height of the summer in water as deep as this. The banks are clear in some parts to allow for easy access to the water's edge. Scrubworms, crickets, frogs and mudeyes are the accepted baits here, while a spinner will also promote some action. Fly-fishing is practised at times, but more often on the Macalister River that feeds the dam. Some particularly big trout may be encountered in the heavy water below the weir when a fair volume is flowing over the spillway. Glenmaggie Camping Park is located in Licola Road, offering powered and unpowered sites, plus showers and toilets, etc, but it is necessary to book in advance during holiday periods. Glenmaggie Reservoir is 215 km east of Melbourne.

## Hopkins River

Found around Warrnambool, this tiny river presents the angler with some remarkably big trout below Ararat, although above that point is hardly worth fishing. From Ararat down to Hexham the river flows through fairly level country over a bed of gravel and mud. Redfin are plentiful but of no great size, and a few eels may also be hooked. It is the brown trout, however, that you seek here, growing to well beyond 3 kg. Below Hexham to the river mouth, big trout are still the quarry, averaging out to about a kilo apiece, but blackfish, more eels, tench and carp, tupong and Australian bass come more into the picture. An 11-km stretch of estuary water runs from the river mouth at Warrnambool to Tooram Stones. The upper reaches yield reasonable wet- and dry-fly-fishing. Baits worth a try are bait-fish, mudeyes and worms worked in a manner to give them more life, which will hopefully prove to be too tempting for the fish to resist. There is access to the water at Warrnambool, Rowans Lake and Jubilee Park. The estuary section produces Australian salmon, mulloway and estuary perch. Stocked with brown trout.

## Jacksons Creek

Jacksons Creek, which is part of the Maribyrnong River basin, is a noted trout and redfin water to be found near Clarkefield. Flowing through grazing country, the bed is of gravel and rock, ideally suited to the good head of brown trout that dominates in this creek. They're not big fish—they reach a weight of about a kilo—but there's plenty of them to offer grand sport on all styles of fishing. During the spring and summer the water used to be a fly-fisherman's paradise, and on occasion returns to its former glory, although it's advisable to fish well upstream of Clarkefield. All species respond well to worms, grubs, perhaps to slugs and, when in season, a grasshopper is perhaps the best of all—fished on the top on a weightless line. Mudeyes presented in a likewise fashion will also be accepted without a qualm. Access is possible from several public roads, and the creek is stocked heavily with brown trout almost annually.

## Kangaroo Lake

Situated between Kerang and Lake Boga, this 882-hectare water is mainly fished for the huge redfin dwelling within its depths. They are expected to be larger than 3 kg, so obviously a bait big enough to arouse the interest of such monsters is the most likely to succeed. Large scrubworms jigged about in the water, bait-fish set just off the bottom, or maybe even a larger-than-normal spinner will be called upon to fool them, but why not try all three? Murray cod, silver and golden perch, tench, bony bream and carp are also reputed to be in the water, to amount to quite a mixed fishery. Thick mats of aquatic weed around the shallows demand the use of a boat here, where picnicking and camping is a part of the scene.

## Kiewa River

Upstream from Mount Beauty the west branch of the Kiewa River flows swiftly through mountainous, thickly wooded country in a series of miniature cascades and rapids as it speeds over the boulder-strewn bed. Once acclaimed the finest dry-fly water in the state, the hydro-electric scheme developed in the area served to unbalance the natural habitation of the insect life that made fly-fishing such a profitable venture. This style of angling is still very much in evidence however, and often absolutely first-class. Cover in the form of shrubbery along the banks affords the angler a suitable hide from which to cast, although wading the stream adds to the delight of pursuing the fish in this most artistic fashion. Greenwell's glory, black ant, butcher, iron blue dun and similar patterns on a size 14 hook are the most successful. Suggested baits are worms, wood grubs and mudeyes, with the grasshopper a firm favourite when it appears on the banks at the height of the summer.

Small brown and rainbow trout abound in most parts of the river, although the east branch upstream from Mount Beauty Pondage is considered inferior to other stretches. Especially downstream from the pondage, where the tobacco crops grow, the brownies also grow—to above 2 kg. The Mount Beauty Pondage is found just outside the town of that name, and contains fair redfin to add to the variety of fishing here. The pondage is a regulating basin in the Kiewa hydro-electricity scheme, and is stocked occasionally with brown trout.

## King River

There is excellent trout fishing on this most popular river that begins its journey high in the heavily-timbered mountain country and passes tobacco fields and grazing land upstream of Moyhu. Abounding with brown trout for most of its length, the river is perfect for all kinds of fishing, from dry-fly to spinning. The top section is devoted mainly to the dry-fly enthusiast, who will use among other patterns the brown nymph, Greenwell's glory and the brown ant. Below Moyhu redfin become more noticeable, with the odd Macquarie perch and Murray cod. But it's the trout fishing that beckons the angler to this water, and above Cheshunt Bridge is rainbow water, where natural bait-casting is perfected to a fine art. Fishing is good throughout most of the year, but it pays to change tactics with each season. When the grasshoppers invade the banks in their millions, for example, then one is used for bait—or a fly resembling it. For the spin-fisher, spoons on the small side are suggested, such as silver wobblers, celtas or similar. The King River is part of the Ovens River drainage system.

## Learmonth Lake
One of a number of lakes in the Ballarat area, this water is of 485 hectares. The predominant species is redfin that go to more than 2 kg. But tench, eels, brown and rainbow trout are there too, the latter often well over 3 kg. The lake is subject to fish mortalities however, so it is no longer stocked regularly. A boat-launching ramp is available and also a camping park.

## Lindsay River
An often neglected breakaway section of the Murray River close to the South Australian border, the Lindsay River contains most of the Murray species, and is therefore similarly subject to closure. Access is gained from an unmade road running parallel to the water—although most of the land in between is private property, it allows the angler to reach the water's edge. Good fishing is obtained here for European carp, which are in abundance, silver and golden perch (the latter to 5 kg), redfin, catfish, crucian carp and a few Murray cod (expected to reach a weight of 4 to 5 kg). Suggested baits are yabbies, mussels, small live bait-fish and grubs, fished on or near the bottom. Larger lures of the flatfish type are recommended for the better fish, along with Flopys. Boat-fishing must afford the best opportunity for success, but good sport is quite possible from the banks.

## Little Murray River
Situated at Swan Hill, the Little Murray is in fact a large river, very similar in appearance to the Murray proper, with much the same fish to be taken, i.e. catfish, Murray cod, blackfish, silver and golden perch, carp, eels and redfin to well over 2 kg. The water maintains a constant level between the Fish Point Regulator and the Little Murray weirs, but beyond these the level gets very low in winter. A boat ramp and picnic area are found near the Little Murray Weir. The best fishing is to be had below and above this weir for a distance of 10 km. Baits and lures applicable to the Lindsay River will work equally well here.

## Macalister River
Running through Maffra, 211 km east of Melbourne, the Macalister is a major Victorian river, containing mainly brown trout but also a few rainbows, that demand the greatest of care when handled on the end of lightweight gear. Above the Glenmaggie Lake the river travels quickly through hilly country in fast runs, bypassing long, deep pools that contain many good fish. The flow decreases as the river becomes wider downstream from Licola, where some brown trout can be tempted on worms, grubs and similar baits, while the rainbows will prefer the upper reaches where the more rapid flow suits their lifestyle better. The best fishing here is to be had during spring and summer. Below Glenmaggie Lake the countryside flattens out to make access more bearable. The trout tend to reach a better size in this section, although redfin appear here more often to compete for the angler's bait. Eels and European carp are also to be had. Immediately below Glenmaggie dam wall some excellent

brownies congregate during the autumn and spring to offer some really worthwhile fishing. Below Maffra the water is affected by effluents from a butter-processing plant during the warmer months and is therefore to be avoided.

## Mallacoota Inlet
This is a large estuary region surrounded by heavily timbered terrain. Bream, flathead, luderick, mullet, trevally, garfish, estuary perch, sand whiting, tailor and mulloway are all to be taken here at times. It is mainly a fishing and tourist resort with all the usual facilities available, including boat-hire and accommodation. Good fishing is possible during the various seasons throughout the year, but June to November is considered the best time for bream, and then on come the flathead until March. Mallacoota is 542 kilometres east of Melbourne.

## Malmsbury Reservoir
A domestic water supply permitting fishing from the bank only. The reservoir contains decent brown trout averaging out at 1 kg, although some taken are twice that size. Large shoals of tiny redfin create something of a nuisance when feeding, but the water is popular and heavily fished. Tench and crucian carp are also present to keep the angler amused. But night-fishing this water produces the best results and a frog fished on the surface at such times will make the effort of forsaking the cot for the night well justified. Malmsbury Reservoir covers an area of 307 hectares, and is found at Kyneton, 84 km north-west of Melbourne.

## Meering Lake
Not a venue for the serious angler but just the place for a family outing. Situated near Kerang, the water offers fishing for European carp, redfin, and a few will-o'-the-wisp Murray cod that have probably been in the water since the year dot. Boating and speedboating are a part of the scene, with boat-ramp and camping facilities on the shore surrounded by farming land. The lake is not large by normal standards, being of a mere 200 hectares, so a spoon trolled from a boat must soon cover most of the water—and those ultra-shy cod.

## Merri River
If the angler is in quest of some titanic trout then here's the place to get them. Fish of more than 4 kg are reputed to reside almost unmolested in the Merri River, and the average catch is at least a kilo, although those who know the water best would insist that most fish taken are well over that weight. The river runs quite close to Warrnambool, 262 km west of Melbourne. Upstream of Woolaston Weir—north of the Princes Highway—numerous brown trout to 2.3 kg are had from the water flowing through thick bush and grazing land, where many pools exist to receive attention from the trout-chaser's flies, lures and baits. Below Woolaston it enters the tidal reaches, in which the biggest trout of all are sought—and claimed to be the finest in south-western Victoria.

The Merri River is the fly-fisher's mecca, where most of the monsters fall victim to flies that seem incredibly tiny in comparison to the fish they're intended to satisfy in terms of a feed. Among the favoured patterns are wet and dry Greenwell's glory, red and black matukas and others of similar design. Baits include worms, mudeyes and small live bait-fish. Small celtas and bright, silver wobblers work well in the clearer swims. A small boat launched at the end of Russells Lane in Dennington will enable the angler to reach the better spots between Warrnambool and Dennington. Night fishing is said to be extremely productive on this water, when the fish leave their haunts to feed in earnest. Estuary fish are apparently scarce here, but the water is stocked heavily with brown trout, and some rainbows are also present, although they don't appear to attain the enormous size of the brownies.

## Mitchell River
Sited at Bairnsdale, the Mitchell River is difficult to reach in some parts (upstream from Glenaladale, for example), but elsewhere access is less of a challenge. Upstream from Lindenow the river flows through heavily timbered hilly country, but below this point the land is flat. In the area of Glenaladale National Park, walking tracks alongside the river allow for easy access to some of the better spots. Brown trout to 2 kg and rainbows to 3 kg could make a visit to the water a most memorable one. The river fishes best in the winter months, when brown trout of up to an incredible 7 kg are said to have been captured from the lower reaches of the water. European and crucian carp are also to be encountered in this section, along with a few bass. The estuary stretch downstream from a boulder barrier established 5 km upstream from Bairnsdale, carries yellow-eyed mullet, estuary perch, luderick, bream and some flathead. The finest trout are said to be taken in the lower reaches between July and August. The area is well catered for in terms of accommodation.

## Mitta Mitta River
Mainly a rainbow and brown trout stream, flowing for most of its length through very hilly country, particularly between the Gibbo River Junction and Larsen Creek. Browns in this area may reach 2 kg, while the rainbows are much smaller. Above the Gibbo River Junction the terrain is similar and so is the size of the fish. From Larsen Creek to Mitta Mitta the trout are joined by redfin, blackfish, and Macquarie perch. Access is difficult in places.

## Lake Modewarre
Rugged, windy, with very little shelter in parts, Lake Modewarre is nevertheless a most popular venue for those who appreciate the full potential of this water.

Located just a few kilometres east of Geelong on the Colac Highway, Modewarre, filled in 1953, was once a most noted fly-water for big rainbow trout, but is now recognised more for the decent brownies and mighty great redfin that predominate there, to be taken on either a bait fished from the bank or a roving spinner from a boat, although a spoon trolled is more likely to tempt a big 'un.

Well stocked with redfin, rainbow and brown trout, the water is slightly brackish. Some huge eels in the lake will also convince the angler battling them to a standstill that he's into the trout of his life.

A great deal of night-fishing during the warmer months takes place here, and those with a frog or cricket fished on the top in the margins stand an excellent chance of getting amongst some really fine fish, but it pays to keep the bait moving a bit to draw attention to its presence there. Possibly there's no better way to fish on a moonlight night. A black matuka representing a mudeye or perhaps a tadpole at night is another way of conning a few nice fish to the net, while mudeye and minnow baits worked deeply at the end of a fly-line are considered by some to be the most killing method of all. It should be remembered, however, that redfin will rarely feed in earnest after dark.

Spinning from the banks also has its followers who depend mainly on the smaller lures, such as a Flopy or celta.

Scrubworms, mudeyes, small bait-fish and large slugs will also coax a few fish to them, and probably the smaller-size yabbie may be added to the list but, whenever possible, it's better to offer the bait on a leadless line or, failing that, try a disappearing sinker. Sugar lumps, chunks of domestic salt, ice cubes with gravel added before setting to help make them sink— all these, once dissolved, will leave nothing but the baited hook to frighten off the fish! Boating facilities are as you find them, but no official camping is permitted here. Five thousand brown and 15 000 rainbow trout were recently released in Lake Modewarre, which is about 30 m deep at its maximum when the level of the lake is at its highest point.

## Moorabool Reservoir
Controlled by the Ballarat Water Commission, from which a permit to fish must be obtained before wetting a line, the Moorabool Reservoir is a domestic water supply basin in which some fine brown trout have become noted for the sport they afford the angler using fly gear. The trout go to well over 2 kg, and although large numbers never figure in the angling here, the fish taken are consistent enough in their behaviour patterns and feeding habits to demand the respect of those who seek them out whenever opportunity allows. Forested country surrounds the lake, and the fish are believed to spawn in the creek flowing into the dam. It also contains small redfin and tench, which must breed here in a natural manner, since no stocking of the water with any species is undertaken, making it self-supporting in this respect. Restrictions applicable to the fishing of all reservoirs will be in force at Moorabool.

## Murdeduke Lake
Murdeduke Lake, located at Winchelsea, is rather a puzzling fishery. Stocked regularly with rainbow trout since 1974, the fishing at first began to gain momentum. Many nice fish began to appear, and something of a reputation was awarded the water by those who fished it regularly. But then mortalities within the dam began to take a heavy toll of the fish-life beneath the surface, to leave some doubts remaining about the future potential of Murdeduke as a reasonable water to fish. The low level of the lake is the accepted reason for the mortalities, and those intending to try their luck are advised to consult the Fisheries and Wildlife Division to see if the venture would be worthwhile.

## Myrtle Creek

Myrtle Creek is a very tiny ribbon of water flowing through grazing land near Harcourt. Access is difficult, being made through private property, but once you are at the water's edge the fishing can produce a few surprises. Brown trout, with the possibility of rainbows, will interest the angler most, although redfin, tench and crucian carp are present too, so any may take the bait. For a water so small, the fish, particularly the brownies, grow to quite a good size, and trout of over a kilo may well present a few problems when taken on the finest of lines. A completely leadless arrangement is bound to succeed where a weighted line will simply take the bait to the bottom and keep it there out of harm's way. Tiny worms, grubs, and other such baits will work if presented in a natural manner.

## Nagambie Lake

A shallow 1807-hectare sheet of water, Nagambie Lake is found close to the township of Nagambie, and supports redfin, catfish, bony bream, crucian carp, tench, brown trout and a few Murray cod. Spinning and bait-fishing are the techniques most widely used on the lake, and redfin appear to be the most dominant species, going to perhaps 2 kg. Open grazing land allows for decent bank fishing, but the best spinning is done from a boat. The Chinamans Bridge Camping Ground offers all the normal facilities but doesn't allow pets. Bookings are necessary for holiday periods. Nagambie Lake is 150 km north of Melbourne.

## Nicholson River

Located at Nicholson, the river flows through heavily forested country above Deptford, but downstream the banks begin to clear enough to make access easier than the situation higher upstream beyond Deptford. The character of the bottom consists of gravel and mud, with boulders in some areas. It carries predominantly brown trout that may reach a kilo, but are generally of a much smaller size. Eels and grayling may also be intercepted well downstream, and below Sarsfield is estuary water, containing bream, mullet, garfish, European carp and a few estuary perch. Normal estuary baits and methods are recommended in the lower reaches of the Nicholson River, while in the upper reaches baits kept on the move score the most bites. Worms, bait-fish, and possibly the smaller type of spinners are the suggested lures and baits, although when it is available local advice should be followed.

## Lake Purrumbete

The best time to arrive at Lake Purrumbete is just on dusk, when illuminations at the moorings burst into life to guide the boats in. A small crowd will then gather to see what's been caught, to offer the newcomer some idea of the huge fish to be taken from this most picturesque water.

The highly esteemed quinnat salmon and rainbow trout are the species to be encountered here, along with some enormous eels that take a bit of eluding when baits are fished on or near the bottom for the salmon. The trout-fisher's offering will normally be nearer the surface—perhaps a mere metre or two below it, suspended from a bubble float that is allowed to drift away from the boat.

Galaxias minnows, that teem in their millions here, are a reliable bait for most of the year, and may be taken in fair numbers at night in either a trap or a finely meshed net. They're also to be had on the tiniest of hooks and floats. Bread dough or tiny fragments of worms are the baits to tempt them and it's a delightful way to spend an hour before bedding-down for the night.

Mudeyes, when available during the spring and summer months, will soon replace the minnows as the favoured baits for both the salmon and trout; they are fished near the surface on a leadless line to permit them to react most enticingly to the movement of the water to encourage more fish to take an interest in them.

However, most trout baits in season will take fish, although fly-fishing is rarely practised on the lake, possibly due to the water's fantastic depth in parts. Quinnat salmon will at times be taken alongside the trout on the same baits; but many anglers prefer to offer these a whitebait instead, fished just off the bottom.

Deep trolling with most familiar lures will also account for many fine fish—especially salmon, and is the method adhered to by those who visit the water regularly. Paravanes are frequently used to keep the lures working deeply.

The reeds in the shallows tend to belie the fact that the lake is very deep in parts. The maximum depth has been charted at 45 metres, and the average at 28 metres. There's a shoreline of 10.3 kilometres, and for the angler afloat that's a lot of water to roam.

Fishing from the bank is possible at several locations, but it's those in the boats who net the biggest number of the better fish. Unfortunately, there are no boats to be hired here, but boat ramps and mooring facilities are absolutely first-class. A charge of $2 annually is expected to help keep them so, and also covers membership to the Lake Purrumbete Angling Club, which allows the angler's catch to be officially weighed and recorded.

Stocking of the lake takes place when necessary to maintain a good head of fish that have an incredible growth rate. Approximately fifty times their initial weight is expected to be gained each year. The water has the unique distinction of holding the world's record for the largest rainbow trout at two and half years, that went approximately 5.8 kg; the best yearling trout, 1.3 kg; the biggest three-year-old rainbow, about 8.3 kg; plus the world's best four-year-old that turned the scales at 8.8 kg.

At the time of writing, many outsize salmon are being removed from the lake before they die to be stripped of eggs to help the breeding programme along.

Close seasons at Purrumbete are variable (often coinciding with recent stockings), so those contemplating a visit should check this matter out first with the Victorian Fisheries and Wildlife Division.

A bag limit of five quinnat salmon per day is in force, although no regulations apply to the trout other than those applicable to waters in general throughout the state. The use of redfin (English perch), carp or tench as bait is prohibited.

Accommodation may be had at the lakeside where a camping/caravan park exists with all the usual amenities, although if a powered site is sought, then the visitor is advised to book one in advance.

## Rocklands Reservoir

Stocked regularly with brown trout, this water, situated near Balmoral, appears to suit the species admirably. Fish of up to 3 kg await the angler who's scientific enough in his approach to con them into accepting his offering without hesitation. Most however must content themselves with fish half this size, because the better ones do demand that extra bit of knowledge, skill and dedication. Redfin appear to be the dominant species here, attaining at best a weight of 2 kg; but rainbow trout, carp, tench and blackfish add to the variety of the fishing. Spinning with large celtas, super dupers, and similar spoons in this huge 6550 hectares of water may perhaps be the best method of dodging the smaller fish and concentrating on the big 'uns. Large baits fished near the bottom should also attract them. Camping facilities will be found at the dam wall.

## Rocky Valley Reservoir

This is the main storage dam of the hydro-electricity scheme in the Falls Creek area; the water is found above the snow-line in the higher snow-grass country. Covering an area of 263 hectares, the dam freezes over during the worst winters, at which time vehicles can only reach the Falls Creek Ski Village. Decent sized brown trout provide the best fishing, although they can be spasmodic at times, due to the fact that this water is no longer stocked, and therefore relies on the fish to spawn in the inflowing streams to maintain a reasonable population of the species. In good weather access is possible by an unsealed mountain road.

## Sydenham Inlet

Sydenham Inlet, near the township of Bemm River, is a shallow estuary consisting of a sandy, muddy bottom, and sheltered by the surrounding brush and forest. It maintains a good head of bream, trevally and estuary perch, plus some decent sized brown trout of normally more than a kilo below the freshwater stretch at the 'Falls'. During the months of June to December the bream anglers arrive in force to take their bag limit of ten per day. It is a popular holiday resort, with camping and cabin facilities available. From the Princes Highway an access road leads to the inlet, which rises tremendously at times when the entrance to the sea is dammed temporarily. Locally obtained baits will normally suffice to bring about the best catches.

## Tarago River

Above Tarago Reservoir the river flows through heavily timbered country and over a gravelly bed. Predominantly a brown trout water, rainbow trout and the occasional blackfish also make an appearance. The browns average out at over a kilo, and may be taken on baits or flies, although for most of the year the bait-fisher's worms, wood grubs, or whatever else may be evident in fair numbers at the time, will be more readily accepted. From the reservoir to the Bunyip River the trout get smaller, and the area is therefore not to be recommended. Tarago Reservoir was until recently a big fish water, with browns and rainbows reaching at least 5 kg, but the water is now closed to the public, unfortunately, and will probably remain so, to the disappointment of those who fished here regularly.

## Thomson River

A swiftly flowing stream above Cowwarr, travelling through hilly, timbered country over a bed of gravel. Situated at Sale, a centre well geared to receive the influx of holidaymakers that converge on the area each summer, the Thomson River contains brown trout to above a kilo, eels and blackfish. Despite the absence of any big fish, the stream is exceedingly favoured by those who come to dabble for the trout. Below Cowwarr the stream slackens in pace to pass banks now lined with willows. The trout, eels and blackfish are now joined by some European carp that will accept most baits fished on the bottom. Dry-fly fishing is also practised in parts by those preferring to wade the stream.

## Wallace Lake

Aquatic weed beds make fishing from the banks rather difficult in some areas of this relatively small sheet of water, so the best results must be expected from a boat, for which a launching ramp is available. Located at Edenhope, the lake supports redfin, tench, rainbow and brown trout, the latter reaching a weight of 2.6 kg. Brown trout are released in the water on a regular basis, so a good stock of fish is always present, and are to be coaxed to the hook on lures trolled slowly or spun from the boat or bank. A good selection of different kinds is suggested so that all may be tried until one is stopped in its tracks by a taking fish. Baits larger than those used on the streams will usually work wonders on still waters, so the biggest of scrubworms is a first choice. Camping facilities will be found at the lakeside.

## Waranga Reservoir

This reservoir, set in level open country near Rushworth, is a massive 5947 hectares, and amounts to a widely mixed fishery. Inhabited mainly by redfin, it also contains the inevitable brown trout, callop, crucian carp, tench, and perhaps even a few Murray cod. With so many species to angle for, techniques must be many. The redfin reach a weight of not less than 2 kg, and each fish taken will be around half that size, so it is claimed, and the best trout will fair a little better. The callop may well grow to around 7 kg, although those taken fall well below that figure. Big baits fished on the bottom around the margins at night will tempt all species excepting the redfin, which are not by nature nocturnal. These, the trout and the callop will fall victim to a large worm or dead fish that is allowed to sink to the bottom without the aid of a sinker and then brought erratically to the top again. Such a technique can be equally effective if done from the bank. Small live fish presented in the normal fashion will also sort out the finest fish of all, as will a spinner in the hands of an angler who knows how to instil life into the lure.

Since the only decent bank fishing is likely to be had around the inlet channels, the best results must be had from a boat. A launching ramp is available for the angler's use. The Waranga Reservoir is a storage basin of the State Rivers and Water Supply Commission; it has an average depth of a mere seven metres, which helps a lot when bait-fishing, if perhaps not when spinning. Under these conditions a bubble float set to dangle the bait just a metre off the bottom might prove to be the most killing method of all, but the bait should be drifted well away from the boat.

### Wartook Reservoir

A well-stocked water containing redfin, blackfish, tench, rainbow and brown trout, it makes for good fishing with lures, flies and baits. The redfin and brownies attain a maximum weight of about 2 kg, while the rainbows are smaller. The latter are more often taken from the centre of the lake, and the browns around the margins. An angling club hut stands near the launching ramp, suggesting that local fishermen may be close at hand to offer their advice on the best spots and tactics, to help the newcomer to net his first fish from here. The reservoir embraces an area of 1031 hectares, and is sited at Halls Gap. Camping and boating is permitted on the lake but no boats are allowed that are powered beyond 10 hp.

### Wellington Lake

This is estuarine water requiring no inland fishing licence. Establish at Sale—the lake is an enormous 14 000 hectares in area, so there's room enough for everyone! European carp growing to about 12 kg or larger are the main species to be encountered here, and are kept company by a few brown trout that are believed to reach a top weight of 5 kg. Bream, mullet, eels and estuary perch are also to be had by those who can manage to forget about those huge brownies. Wellington Lake is the shallowest, but also the largest of the Gippsland Lakes, and is therefore well patronised by those who flock to this scene each summer. Local baits, methods and rigs are suggested for those new to the water, which is as different from stream fishing as cheese is from chalk.

### Wendouree Lake

One of a number of useful waters in the area of Ballarat, Wendouree Lake is shallower than most, and therefore carries a lot of weed. The lake is subject to closure during June and July each year to allow for liberations of tiny trout to settle in a little before becoming the hunted prey of the angler's various methods of extracting them from their new environment. Most survive to the kilo mark, while others manage twice that size, to cause something of a sensation when finally fooled into playing the angler's game. Both brown and rainbows are present, plus redfin, tench and carp, although it's the trout that carry the largest numbers. Both types of trout are released at regular intervals into this water to maintain a good head of fish. Small power boats are allowed on the lake and most accepted techniques will take fish.

### Werribee River

A tiny stream running through Bacchus Marsh, it offers little worthwhile fishing for most of its length. However, downstream from Melton Reservoir may hold a few surprises for the angler prepared to sit and catch a few of the tiny roach that inhabit the shallows, and then use them for bait. Some fairly big brown trout reside in the river at this point, unsuspected even by most of the locals, who will rarely if ever try a live roach, which appears to be the only bait to bring the trout out of hiding. Quite a few years ago now, some excellent redfin were taken on the same baits in the water cascading over the tiny dam wall, but have since disappeared—perhaps for good.

## Yambuk Lake

A small estuary lake consisting of a mere 80 hectares in size, it is nevertheless a popular fishing and boating venue. Situated at Yambuk, the lake taking its name is, as to be expected, dominated by estuarine species of fish, including good numbers of salmon, mullet, bream and estuary perch, which are taken on whitebait, shrimps, minnows, crabs and spew worms. But the ever-present brown trout is also in residence, with a few tupong, eels and tench. The lake is formed by the Shaw and Eumeralla rivers merging as one to create the estuary, and the trout wander from these rivers to join the fish in the lake. Sheltered to a degree by the surrounding sand dunes, the angler may fish from a boat or the bank, but should seek local advice about the best tactics to fish the best spots at the most likely time to succeed.

The Craigs and Cape Remeur are by far the most noted rock-fishing quarters in the entire area, producing at times good flathead, mulloway, sharks of various descriptions and even a few yellow-tail kingfish. Reasonable sport can be had at most points throughout the year, particularly where the rivers enter the lake and where that in turn flows into the sea. Access is possible to the lower reaches of the rivers via the lake proper, and the angler investigating their potential will be pleased to learn that the brown trout grow to above 2 kg. Yambuk Lake is to be reached after a 320-kilometre drive west of Melbourne, a journey many make in order to experience the variety of fishing to be obtained here, and the mixture of different species that add so much to it. The usual camping facilities will be discovered at the lake.

## Yarra River

From the foothills of the Great Dividing Range in the north, the Yarra and its tributaries flow through a wide variety of riverside scenery. It's a deep, lazy river nearer the city, gliding unhurriedly through lush meadows to rendezvous with the sea.

To the angler trotting a tiny quill float along in its path, to intercept the good quality roach that abound in vast numbers where the stream slackens to a steady flow, there is perhaps no other river quite like it. Yet big redfin, large European carp, monster eels, the odd trout or two, and even the occasional Murray cod are there also, awaiting attention from those prepared to fish this water as seriously as any other.

Each weekend anglers in their thousands head for the hills and the higher streams when they've so much forgotten water at home—on their very doorsteps in fact, for the River Yarra is undoubtedly the most underrated fishery in the state! But the fish are there, completely unsuspected by those who turn up their noses at the potential it offers.

No fewer than six large reservoirs are served by the Yarra, but none is open to the angling public, unfortunately, which is a great pity because each in its own way would add much to our sport. But we've plenty of scope without them, both in variety of fish and fishing styles.

Below the Upper Yarra Reservoir the main flow sweeps swiftly through densely wooded country to create small rapids and pools containing fair numbers of brown trout. They're small but lively fish, responding well to a tiny dry fly, such as a brown ant, red tag or coachman. Wet flies include Alexandra, coachman and Watson's fancy. A tiny worm on the smallest of hooks will also make contact, but should be fished without any lead on the line where possible to allow the flow of the stream to carry it along to the fish in the natural paths of the currents. Gossamer line is a necessity here, and a kilo in strength isn't too fine for what after all are very tiny trout, rarely attaining a size big enough to bust the line, unless the angler is heavy-handed with them. A road runs parallel with the river to make access to it easy.

From Warburton through to Lilydale the river continues to travel at a rapid flow, passing grazing land to add to the picturesque setting. The bottom is sandy, but becomes rather muddy near Healesville, and where there's mud in the Yarra there's also bound to be eels, some of enormous size as the river slackens nearer the sea. In this stretch the pools get larger and so do the trout in them, but as they grow bigger the number tends to decrease. Redfin, roach, carp, eels and even the elusive blackfish may be part of the catch here, but the prize of course is a nice brownie. Some are said to reach a weight of over 3 kg here, although news of such fish rarely leaks out—which isn't to say they're not taken! The area around Healesville is regularly stocked with the species, so the angler shouldn't shun the possibility of getting amongst them.

As the flow picks up speed to pass through Lilydale and on to Warrandyte the banks become steep enough in parts to make access to the water difficult, but flatten out again nearer the city. At Wonga Park there's still a mixed bag of fish to be had by those prepared to think a little about the best way to catch them. The tiny roach close into the edge are a first-rate bait not just for the redfin and eels but also for the few big trout that stalk the water close into the banks. Like most of the better fish, these remain almost unmolested by the fishing fraternity who refuse to acknowledge their presence in the Yarra, particularly as it nears Melbourne. But the trout are in residence nevertheless—not in their hundreds by any means, but most certainly by the score—and they're not tiny fish either!

Most come out to feed at night, and the dead-fish bait of the eeling angler will occasionally be taken by a trout instead. Imagine then, if you will, just what the results might be if you fished for trout especially at night. Don't fish with worms, because they quickly become eel-fodder; try instead a small live fish on the bottom, or failing that a lively frog on the top. There are a few surprises in store for the angler out on the banks of the Yarra at night. The eels alone are worthy of such a venture, but don't expect to get the big ones on worms—a dead fish is what they're after, and there's no mistaking the indications on the rod that they've got it. They'll take the rod also if allowed to, which means the recovery arm of the reel must be left open to let them have line.

The bait-fish can be had easily enough by using tiny hooks and small pellets of bread dough or pieces of worm. A small quill float will let the bait-snatcher know when to strike as it disappears, but don't be surprised if a big carp takes the bait instead, because there's plenty in the lower reaches of the Yarra—and they are big!

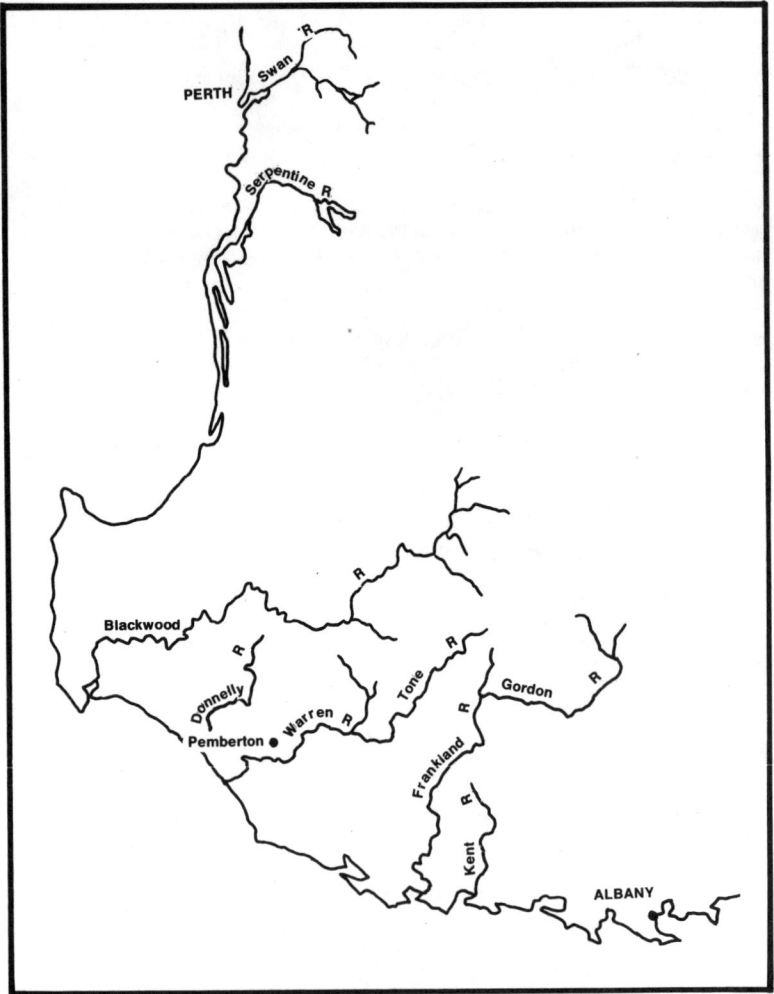

**WESTERN AUSTRALIA (SOUTH)**

# WESTERN AUSTRALIA

To head out west is for some just as long a journey as to go north, without the added stimulus of the exotic species of the top end. Yet often overlooked is the fact that Western Australia has its own top end, the Kimberley. Credited with being the last fishing frontier in the land, the resources of the north-west haven't yet been fully investigated. But word is out about the giant barramundi being taken from the Fitzroy River, and that's just one of the species normally associated with Queensland that are met in the Kimberley area.

Trout fisheries out west are no longer a myth, but a functioning certainty. And the size the trout grow to might surprise a few. Both rainbows and browns are to be taken in the south-west, as proof enough of the stocking programmes that have over the years brought their reward. In fact the state has developed its own speciality, a rainbow known as the Westralian, that can endure better the higher temperatures to be experienced in the west. Browns fare a little worse than rainbows, but over all both trout have settled in nicely.

Yet it was not without a great deal of effort that trout were established in Western Australia, as well as the rest of the country. Attempts originally began in 1874 to introduce trout to the western state, but not until 1936 did a spark of promise emerge. During that year a small hatchery on the Lefroy Brook in the region of Pemberton, 348 kilometres south of Perth, successfully hatched a shipment of eggs from Ballarat; these were reared and later released in waters ranging between Gin Gin and Albany. The rest is history, for which the trout-chaser can be thankful. Constant stocking is necessary to keep the waters filled with trout, but that applies to the waters of many states.

The Murray River (not to be confused with the mighty Murray) flowing south of Perth is a good trout fishery, and quite noted for the sport it provides. In the Waroona district there is a dam by the same name and that, too, is a trout fishery, lending itself very well to the fly-fishermen who find that here a good population of insect life exists for the trout, while on other waters they're somewhat lacking.

Each inland district of the south-west has, or is working on the development of, trout fishing. It has perhaps been more difficult to establish the species in a region that is technically unsuitable; so our appreciation of the effort involved should be more profound. Redfin, introduced at the turn of the century, are climatically settled well enough by now to be self-supporting in number without any outside help. Since most native fish in the south-west are inferior in size to the alien species, it is indeed fortunate that they are there, otherwise the entire vast area would provide poor freshwater fishing. The scene began to wane in the sixties, but is gaining momentum again.

The fish have always been up in the Kimberley, yet it is only in more recent seasons that the full potential of the fresh waterways there have been realised by the few who have ventured forth to tap it. Already in their wake have come others, taking full advantage of each new kilometre of road pushing through the bush. Some say that because of this the fishing is already beginning to suffer—so those keen to sample the sport available within this area had better not hesitate too long.

## THE NORTH-WEST

On a map the area at the tip of Western Australia known as the Kimberley doesn't look impressive at all. But it covers 363 000 square kilometres, and that's a lot of land. It is to a large extent a sandstone plateau. On the east and south sides, barrier ranges surrender to the Ord and Fitzroy rivers. These waters were, and still are, up to a point; virgin. Indeed, it wasn't until 1960 that a four-year mapping programme of the area was completed; serious inroads into the region haven't yet begun, although I fear that isn't far away.

From a fishing point of view the Kimberley still retains some of its mystic allure for those who dream of faraway places yet never actually get to see them. It's not completely untouched by civilisation—few places can claim that—but several abortive attempts at settlement had to take place before the land was tamed in the late 1880s. Irrigation schemes on the Ord and Fitzroy rivers eventually made possible the cultivation of cotton, rice, sugar cane and other crops that are still flourishing in part to this day. The beef cattle industry is of major importance to the area—but to us it's the fishing that counts.

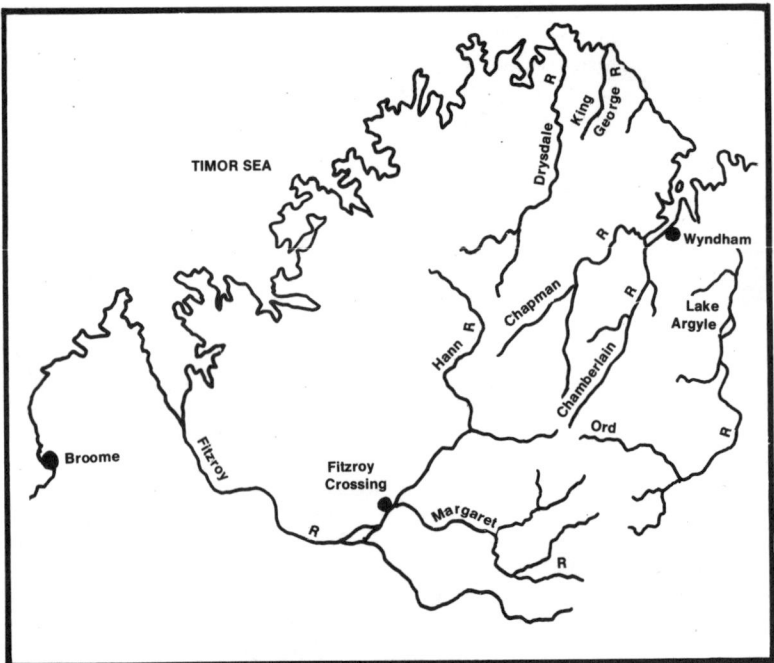

## WESTERN AUSTRALIA (NORTH-WEST)

The Kimberley is scarred with rivers that race through the land without a moment to spare at the height of the wet season, and yet in the dry not even a breeze will stir them. They're tropical waters containing barramundi, big catfish, oxeye tarpon and native perch, to mention but a few of the species met there. But despite this age of the Concord aircraft and atomic submarines, accessibility to the rivers in the north-west is still very much a problem. Not one in ten waters can be reached without the use of a four-wheel-drive. Perhaps one in twenty might be possible, so take note if you intend to go.

## LAKES AND RIVERS

### Lake Argyle

Lake Argyle on the Ord River is described in travel brochures as being a vivid blue water in contrast to the reds and browns of the surrounding cliffs and gorges. Now if that doesn't fire the imagination then nothing will! It's a huge water, said to be many times the size of Sydney Harbour. Water sports of all kinds are enjoyed on the lake, at the bottom of which is the old Argyle Downs Homestead, or rather the site where it stood. The actual building has been re-erected at the top of the dam to retain its link with the past. An attempt was made to farm barramundi at the dam, but was not successful. The suggestion has now been put forward to experiment with the introduction of Nile perch instead. This species is closely related to the barramundi, and is a highly respected freshwater fighter. Unfortunately the characteristics of the barramundi make it an unsuitable candidate for the dam, but catfish, sooty grunter, archer-fish and others combine to make the water a mixed fishery. High above the waters of the lake is the Lake Argyle Holiday Village, which is completely self-contained with a general store and even a restaurant. Bus tours operate from the village, and bush walks and cruises on the dam are a popular pastime here.

### Fitzroy River

The Fitzroy River and its tributaries drain the southern section of the Kimberley area. During the wet season the river floods to cover a wide area, and during the dry it is reduced to a series of waterholes. Rising in the Kimberleys, the Fitzroy River heads west for the Indian Ocean at King Sound. Snags and sand bars have prevented regular navigation of the river. Tributaries include the Hann and Margaret rivers and the Geegully and Christmas creeks. Access is made to the Fitzroy River from Willare Bridge, Langey Crossing and from Broken Wagon Pool. It's a wild, isolated river containing among other creatures huge crocodiles. But as it is the most westerly water in the monsoonal region, it represents the western limit of these amphibians, and also the barramundi. Where possible fishing can be done from the banks, but the angler with a boat will accumulate the better bags of fish.

### Ord River

In the north-west, 106 kilometres from Wyndham, is the centre of the Ord River Scheme. Here the waters of the Ord River are held captive by the diversion dam to form Lake Kununurra. Adjacent to the lake is the township of Kununurra, believed to be the only town to be built in the Kimberley this century. Offering accommodation in first-class hotels as well as caravan parks, the town is well adapted to receive any number of tourists. On the lake is fishing, sailing, swimming and skiing. The Ord River also enters Lake Argyle through densely wooded hills. Rising in the Albert Edward Ranges near the Northern Territory border, the Ord River flows north into the Cambridge Gulf. Tributaries are the Panton, Nicholson, Elvire, Stirling, Wilson, Bow and Denham rivers. The Ord travels through a valley flanked by magnificent scenery. The fish to be expected are the same as those found in Argyle Lake. Tactics used to lure them will vary little from those employed for the same species in Queensland. But when in doubt ask the local fishermen.

**Other Waters**
Beyond the Great Sandy Desert of the north-west region other rivers leave their pattern on the land—the Lannard, Margaret, Hann, Chapman, Pentecost, Gibb and Durack rivers, and most contain those typically northern species: catfish, sleepy cod, longtoms, eels, archer-fish, oxeye tarpon, black grunters—the list is virtually endless. And in no way do they need the help of man to survive and multiply. They manage quite nicely on their own, and have done so since long before we ever came on the scene.

## FISHING IN THE KIMBERLEY

The barramundi is found in every major waterway of the north-west, as well as in the large inland dams and billabongs that have access to them. The Ord and Fitzroy rivers offer the best chances of getting into the barra, and are two of the more easily reached. Plenty of movement in the water during or after the monsoons is suggested as the most likely period in which to make contact with these fish, which restricts the fishing to just three months—March, April and May—and that's just the time to combat the worst possible weather, of course. But didn't somebody once say that life wasn't meant to be easy?

For bait the locals stick fairly rigidly to live fish, be they archer-fish, mullet, tiny oxeye herring or whatever; they are allowed to roam about without too much lead holding them back. Frogs will also tempt them, as will other creatures of a similar size. But various lures will also get into the act, with flatfish and wobblers being perhaps two of the most popular.

The fork-tail catfish are on a lesser plane than the great barramundi, but are more often encountered. They'll accept almost anything for bait provided it is of a meaty substance. They're not great fighters except when taken on the finest of lines. The fish can be palatable after a good deal of preparation. They may be had to over 10 kg.

The black grunter represents a tasty dish, and is regularly taken from the Ord and Fitzroy rivers. It doesn't grow to any great size—a fish of a kilo is a good 'un—but they're good fun to handle on lightweight gear nonetheless, and are pursued mainly with bits of meat on the hook. Another tiny fish, the archer- or rifle-fish, appears to materialise everywhere in the freshwaters of the Kimberley, and are lured on tiny flies or spinners. But ultra-fine lines are again called for to permit them to show their true worth.

The longtom of the freshwater scene is related to its saltwater cousin, although is in reality an individual species. These are again small, attaining at best a weight of about 2 kg. They're amusing little blighters to catch on small live fish and other baits. Tiny spinners will also account for a few, as will equally tiny flies. But longtoms are difficult fish to hook, thanks to the bony beaks they're endowed with. The Ord River and tributaries are where most longtoms are sought, and catching them amounts to a lot of fun.

The oxeye tarpon spans a wide area up in the Kimberley, from as far south as the Ashburton River to well beyond the Ord in the north. Although a game little fighter in its own right, the species is most often caught as bait for barramundi. It may be had approaching 2 kg but the majority are nearer bait-size. Both lures and bait are employed to tackle them, but small spinners are considered to have a slight edge over baits.

The tiniest of all the smaller species in the Kimberley district must surely be the spangled perch, also known as rock trout. It also happens to be the most common. Indeed, wherever there's water there is bound to be spangled perch. They're right little scavengers, having a go at almost anything in the water, even our toes if we aren't too careful, so obviously these little perch demand the least skill to catch them by the dozen.

Many other smaller varieties of fish are to be encountered in the north-west of the state, most of which are of little interest to us except in the form of baits for the better fish in the Kimberley. Some have yet to see an angler's hook up there, and probably never will. For that's the situation in the vast, northern area of the western state, and it's not likely to change in our time.

## TINY TOWNSHIPS OF THE NORTH-WEST

### Fitzroy Crossing
A store, post office, police station, hotel and an Australian Inland Mission Hospital are all part of the town that marks the crossing over the Fitzroy River. A bit out of the way to be termed a tourist attraction, the town nevertheless does enjoy its share of tourists, many of whom during the winter months take a cruise on Geikie Gorge. The gorge, 19 km from the township, consists of towering limestone cliffs over the river below. Barramundi can be had in the Fitzroy River, along with other varieties of fish. But far more interesting to most perhaps are the Johnston crocodiles with which the river abounds. Near the township is an Aboriginal mission.

### Halls Creek
Found between Derby and Wyndham, Halls Creek has the usual facilities of the towns up north: stores, an hotel, garage, police station, post office and caravan park. It's a good town in which to linger awhile, or to leave for the south-east to visit the Wolf Creek Meteorite Crater, 133 km away. A camping area is found at the crater for those who wish to linger some more. Fourteen kilometres from Halls Creek some native missions may be visited.

### Wyndham
Wyndham is Western Australia's most northerly port, and an important base for the angler after barramundi. Found on the Cambridge Gulf, Wyndham is linked with Kununurra by a reasonable road that passes breathtaking scenery. Wyndham is also the port of the Ord River irrigation area.

# THE SOUTH-WEST

## TROUT FISHING

It is said that the present-day trout fishing scene began because a teacher with a bit more interest in his job than some decided to use as a subject for a project with his class of boys the hatching and rearing of trout eggs, these to be placed in the local streams around the tiny township of Pemberton, 348 km south of Perth. So successful was the experiment that it blossomed. It's a strange tale, but one well documented. And because of it anglers in Western Australia now have trout fishing to be proud of. While fishing may be had throughout the year in the irrigation dams, an experimental close season is now in force on the rivers and creeks. This applies to the period May to August, although at the time of writing angling is allowed during these months on the Blackwood, Donnelly, Murray and Warren rivers.

One peculiarity of the fishing here is that the hatches of insects experienced in other states do not occur at all as regularly, so that fly fishing is not accepted as the method supreme here. Indeed, at one stage fly-fishing gear was impossible to obtain, simply because sporting stores could see no point in stocking a commodity that gathered dust and cobwebs on the shelves. But the situation is changing slightly now, and a few intrepid anglers are beginning to learn that the trout out west will in fact rise to a fly when given the chance, so we can expect this technique to develop further in the near future.

The rivers and streams in the west are equal to those elsewhere in the bountiful supply of trout that most carry, although they're deeper than most, and are therefore not to be waded safely. Access to many is still a problem, though not to the extent experienced in the north-west. The large Waroona Dam is easily reached, and is something of a novelty in that here prolific hatches of insects take place each summer, and then some terrific trout fishing is to be had on fly gear. Some 2000 rainbows are lifted from the water each year, averaging out at about a kilo apiece, although some weigh much more. The dam is ideally situated for a holiday, with all the facilities of home, including a camping area, caravan park and even a kiosk.

Another dam, the Samson, is found to the west of Waroona, but is easily overlooked. The Samson Dam contains a fair stock of both rainbows and browns, and affords the visiting angler some memorable sport. A series of spawning streams enter the dam to assure us of a well-stocked larder. If the angler can surmount all barriers to reach the nearby Samson and McKnoe brooks, he'll find excellent trout fishing here too.

South of Perth is the Murray River, the nearest to the city that can be classified as a first-rate fishery for trout. To get at the fish we reach the river by the Murray Valley and Park roads that follow the river. A point upstream called Toms Crossing is claimed to be an excellent spot for trout, as is Island Pool, and wherever the Yarragill, Davis, Swamp Oak brooks and others team up with the Murray. Here again the average rainbow is a kilo, but can be taken twice that size.

The Metropolitan Water Supply dams in the area between Mundaring and Pinjarra are closed to all anglers but, in the downstream reaches of the Serpentine River, above the Serpentine Falls, a few trout are always to be had, as is the case with its tributary known as Cooralong Brook. Enmeshed in private property is Dirk Brook. Permission must be sought to fish it, but the effort is normally well worthwhile, for the Dirk Brook is a better trout stream by far than the Serpentine or its offspring.

Within the Harvey district we find the Harvey Weir—just 2 km east of the Harvey township. The browns here tend to evade the angler's attempts to remove them. The rainbows are more than obliging, however, and help the angler to keep his cool. Logue Brook Dam is 9 km north of Harvey and contains many healthy rainbows. Facilities here are splendid, including a well-served caravan park and camping ground.

While returning to the east of the town again we discover the Stirling Dam, on the Harvey River and upstream from the weir. A few spawning streams enter this river to give it that extra boost of lively wild fish lacking in other waters. It's a difficult river to fish, however, because of the presence of snags. But as any angler worth his salt will know, wherever snags are to be found so are fish. That's a certainty to be taken advantage of. The river itself is worth a bit more trouble to fish, because some extra-large fish are taken from it each year, going to well beyond the 2-kg mark. So don't be beaten by a few snags—get in and fish amongst them.

The Brunswick River demands regular re-stocking of trout to replace those lost when the river ceases to flow at a time of drought, and therefore the head of fish it carries is a bit haphazard. But the Collie River is more promising. Downstream from the Wellington Dam the trout fishing is exceptionally good in the broken water.

Another fine trout stream is the Blackwood River, producing fish of at least a kilo each, but frequent re-stocking is again necessary to maintain the standard of fishing. With its tributaries, such as Ellis Brook, Hesters, Norlup and Shepherds brooks, the Blackwood River is just about the most extensive trout fishery in the state. Other adjacent streams worth visiting are the Arthur, Beaufort, Balgarup and Kojonup rivers.

The finest trouting of all is claimed by some to be exactly where it all began, and this is around the Pemberton area. Here the State Government operates the Pemberton Trout Hatchery, and the region is held as the centre of the south-west freshwater fishing scene. Trout from the hatchery serve the rivers and streams from Perth to Albany, and there are literally dozens of these. Among the best must be added the Warren River, which is really only fishable during the spring and summer due to its thick, brownish water that is too heavy to tackle during the months of winter.

The Donnelly River is particularly acclaimed for its trout fishing. Just 16 km from Pemberton, the Donnelly holds the distinction of having produced the best trout in Western Australia, although the actual weight of the fish is difficult to ascertain. Lures, baits and flies used are much the same as those used in other states. So the belief that Western Australia has no trout is now exploded. They've some beauts!

## OTHER INTRODUCED SPECIES

Apart from the successful transition of trout to the rivers and streams of Western Australia, many other outsiders have been through the acclimatisation process to emerge in triumph. Roach, redfin, tench, carp, Murray cod and callop were all put through the mill at one time or another in the south-west, even the massive Indian gourami, that may grow to nearly two metres, although this last, along with a few other shots at tampering with nature, amounted to nothing at all. Yet other introduced species flourished beyond imagination, those noteworthy being redfin and carp—and of course the trout that came along later.

These foreign fish now dominate the freshwaters of the south-west, where previously there was little sporting content at all. Their placement over the years has created the minimum of upheaval among the few native fish present, and none among those of a sporting nature because they didn't exist, unlike in the other states.

Nowadays, whether they're wanted or not, European carp are abundant in water-filled pits and rivers around Perth, and the smaller and more ornate crucian carp is to be found in the Canning and Helena rivers, among others, and serve to keep the kids happy.

Redfin have settled in remarkably well, as it was assumed they would, for they're hardy fish, and no mean adversary on the end of a fine line— though most anglers seeking them will insist on killing the sport they offer by hauling them in on gear that even a barramundi would object to. Firmly established in the Collie, Harvey, Blackwood, Tone and Warren rivers, the redfin is now in the south-west to stay. And given just half a chance, it'll prove its presence there a great asset when the trout won't oblige, and sometimes when they will, being taken alongside them.

# A WORD ON CONSERVATION

Conservation—that's a word I never heard mentioned during my schooldays, so presumably the people at the time thought there wasn't a need to use such a word. How shamefully wrong they were. It was due to their ignorance that my generation knew nothing about conservation, resulting in the calamity we experience today. Yet they in turn can blame those who taught them . . .

However, despite the mumbling and grumbling to the contrary, the notion of conservation is at last catching on. It still has a long way to go, but slowly but surely we're getting there; perhaps progress is more in areas beyond Australian shores, but even in Australia it must come eventually.

It's no secret that the salmon are running up the River Thames again. Such a simple statement gives little indication of the enormity of such an achievement. The salmon left the Thames several lifetimes ago, in an era when conservation didn't even extend to the human race, let alone to the scaly breed. So I, my father, and his father before him were denied the right to experience this superfish on the end of a line in England. Indeed, for the best part of my lifetime the nearest I have been able to come to a salmon has been in a tin can. Yet now they're running up the Thames again.

The mighty Thames is not a tiny river, yet by world standards it is not enormous. The Murray, in fact, is longer. But the Thames is a very busy river, used not only by pleasure craft but by huge, ocean-going cargo ships and liners and of course it flows through one of the world's major cities. So considerable effort was involved in cleaning it up.

For many decades now it has been an offence for factories to dump their waste in the waters of the United Kingdom, though the penalty was never more than a fine of a few thousand pounds, which to most companies amounted only to a token smack on the wrist. But then an organisation called the Anglers' Co-operative Association (the ACA), gathered the bulk of the fishing clubs around it and fought those who dared tamper with the water. With the backing of several million anglers, the ACA took on allcomers at its own expense, causing the penalty for contaminating any water to leap to hundreds of thousands of pounds—and there the seed was sown in an endeavour to halt the pollution and coax the salmon back to the Thames.

Other factors were of course involved, but without the protest made by that mighty army of anglers the River Thames would today be even more of a sewer than it was yesterday. And here is the direction our own course must take, if we in our turn are to save the streams of Australia.

It takes money. But more than that it demands that we bang on a few doors to make them open to our plight. And this must be done shortly or all will be lost. We are already aware of the diminishing presence of our native fish. Are they to disappear completely, before we make a united stand? Let's fight the industries that dare pollute our rivers and streams. We may then in time turn the clock back to the days when Australian anglers didn't have to travel halfway across the country to find decent sport.

And we must play our own part by being a little more concerned about the fish we take. I have only just been shown a photograph of a very proud angler with more than twenty fine trout displayed at his feet—all dead. While such slaughter continues we haven't a hope of achieving anything. Even the purest of waters can't take that kind of abuse for long. No one needs so many fish. Certainly it's hard to return a good fish to the water when nobody else has seen it, but if our sport is to survive to the extent we envisage, then more consideration must be given to returning fish. The angler should of course retain a few fish for his supper, because that is his right; but twenty? That depletion affects the sport of those following in his wake.

The English have for years enjoyed pitting their skill against each other. A large section of the angling population there takes part in matches each week—in fact, it is the only kind of angling that some of them have experienced. They enjoy what they do immensely which, in a nutshell, is to catch as many tiny fish as they can. These are then dropped into a huge keepnet and weighed-in at the end of the day, after which the fish are returned to the water. True, it's not everyone's idea of sport-fishing, but the competitions did no harm—or so it was thought.

However, now a great storm is gathering; the question has at last been raised about the damage being done to those young fish. They are roughly handled to get the hook out quickly, so another can be caught; while they are kept in a net all day they have their protective slime and scales removed through rubbing up against each other and the mesh of the net; as well, the mesh tears their fins to shreds when they become entangled in it.

We don't stoop to keeping fish in nets in Australia—we simply kill them on the spot, which to my mind is much worse. This habit is made even more distasteful when dead and obviously under-sized fish are presented at the weigh-in, an all-too-frequent practice. If the culprits were disqualified out-of-hand for their offence against nature, this practice would soon come to an end.

However, in Victoria and most other states this unsporting fraction of fishermen within our midst are legally, if not morally, within their rights because there exists there no minimum size limit. Such a situation, if allowed to continue, will ruin our fishing completely. It doesn't automatically follow, however, that if we keep the big fish and let the little ones go all will be well beneath the surface. It is, after all, the bigger fish that have proved their ability to survive by attaining such a size, so they must be the best breeders. (I like to call them members of the super-strain because, in a sense, that's exactly what they are.) And if we return them to their own domain once we've shown them we're just a wee bit smarter, they'll repay us in full by producing offspring that will be, like the parent fish, capable of surviving to a ripe old age. A fish dumped on a plate or a board is of no further use to us.

It can be argued that in some waters the fish wouldn't have spawned in any case because it was itself a hatchery release to a water fully dependent upon artificial re-stocking. Any angler who asks why such a fish should be returned has never in his life put back a really good one, otherwise he'd appreciate the meaning behind the action.

It was a proud moment when I once released a brown trout of well over 3 kg. At the time I worked in a boarding school for backward boys in the West Country of England, and this fish, one among the few remaining in a lake by the school, was often spotted by the boys, and spurred them on to make even greater efforts to catch one for themselves. And the one I caught was greater efforts to catch one for themselves. And the one I caught was probably the biggest and possibly the last of the lot, since none had been seen for ages. But in no way were the lads going to be deprived of the pleasure of seeing that beauty again, cruising near the surface taking in the flies. Yet quite apart from that all-important point, the fish had given me a wonderful time as it battled for its freedom. As soon as it was beaten I knew it was going back. That much it deserved for the great joy it brought me. A lump formed in my throat as I nursed my fish in the shallows until it managed to take off for the deeper water under its own steam. The regret that came when I discovered that same fish dead on the bottom at the other side of the lake the next day has never left me; I'll always carry fond memories of that brief but unforgettable encounter.

Perhaps in a sense this, and not the selfish attitude of making sure there's something left for our pleasure, is what conservation is really about: having a genuine respect for an opponent which merely wishes to live out its life in peace and harmony, just as we ourselves desire to. Mightn't it be a nice gesture to allow it to do just that, in appreciation of the sheer delight it has brought us? Few reasonable men can argue with that suggestion, because it upholds the virtue of a true sportsman and angler.

# CAMPING AND CARAVAN PARKS

## NEW SOUTH WALES AND AUSTRALIAN CAPITAL TERRITORY

### CENTRAL WESTERN DISTRICT

**ABERCROMBIE CAVES Caravan Park and Camping Area,** 2 km from Bathurst–Goulburn Rd; 4 Cabin Vans; bbq; on-site shopping; children's area; pets allowed.

**CANOWINDRA Caravan Park,** Tilga St; 2 on-site vans; local shopping; washing facilities; pets allowed.

**COWRA Cowravan Park,** Lachlan St; 8 on-site vans; pets allowed.

**COWRA DISTRICT Wyangala Dam Recreation Area;** 16 on-site vans; pets allowed.

**FORBES Forbes Country Club,** Sam St; powered sites; 3 on-site vans; washing facilities; on-site shopping; pets allowed.

**FORBES River Meadows Caravan Park,** cnr Newell Hwy and River Rd; powered/unpowered sites; 7 on-site vans; bbq; washing facilities; pets allowed.

**Apex Park,** adjoining Lachlan River, on Cowra Rd; powered/unpowered sites; bbq; children's playground; pool; pets allowed.

**Lachlan View,** 145 Flint St; 8 cabin vans & 11 on-site vans; bbq; playground; on-site shopping; no pets.

**LAKE CARGELLIGO Caravan Park,** Naradhan St; powered/unpowered sites; pets allowed.

**MOLONG Caravan Park,** cnr Watson and Hill Sts; powered sites; local shopping; pets allowed.

**OBERON Camping Reserve,** Cunningham St; powered/unpowered sites; check for on-site vans and pets.

**OBERON DISTRICT** Natural camp sites; At low level bridge over Duckmaloi River on Old Hampton–Oberon Rd;

At Little River, Porters Retreat, 42km from Oberon on the Goulburn Rd;

Abercrombie River, Bummaroo Bridge, 72 km from Oberon on the Goulburn Rd.

**ORANGE Canobolas Caravan Park,** Bathurst Rd; 13 on-site vans; check about pets.

**Showground Caravan Park,** cnr Margaret St and Leeds Pde; powered/unpowered sites; 9 on-site vans; pets allowed.

**ORANGE DISTRICT Lake Canobolas Camping Ground,** 11 km west of Orange check about on-site vans; no pets.

### HUNTER DISTRICT

**CLARENCETOWN Williams River Bridge Reserve,** Duke St; pets allowed.

**DUNGOG Caravan Park** (bank of Williams River); pets allowed.

**FORSTER Forster Camping Reserve,** nr lake entrance and beach; 4 on-site vans; no pets.

**Lani's Caravan Park,** 33 The Lakes Way; 10 on-site vans; pets allowed.

**Sun Coast Caravan Park,** 2 km S Forster-Tuncurry Bridge; 9 on-site vans; pool.

**Smuggler's Cove Caravan Park,** 19 The Lakes Way; 6 cabin vans & 8 on-site vans; pets allowed.

**GLOUCESTER Caravan Park,** 4 cabin vans & 4 on-site vans; pets allowed.

**LAKE GLENBAWN State Recreation Area;** no pets.

**MAYFIELD WEST Walsh's Caravan Park,** Maitland Rd; 15 on-site vans; no pets.

**MUSWELLBROOK Pinaroo Caravan Park,** New England Hwy; 6 cabin vans; 7 on-site vans; bbq; playground; pool; tennis; pets allowed.

**SOLDIERS POINT Caravan Park;** water frontage; no pets.

**TUNCURRY Tuncurry Beach Caravan Park,** Beach St; 5 cabin vans & 10 on-site vans; no pets.

**Great Lakes Caravan Park,** Baird St on Walli Lake; 6 cabin vans & 12 on-site vans; pool; no dogs.

**The Old Dutch Holiday and Caravan Park,** South St; 17 on-site vans; pool; no pets.

**Ne-Lan-Gra Lodge,** South St; 25 on-site vans; pool; no pets.

## MURRAY DISTRICT

**ALBURY Noreuil Park,** Hume Hwy; 2 km N of Albury; 23 on-site vans; no pets.

**Caravanna,** 443 Hume Hwy, Lavington; 9 cabin vans & 17 on-site vans; no pets.

**Albury Tourist Haven,** Hume Hwy; 3 cabin vans & 14 on-site vans; no pets.

**North Albury Caravan Park,** 372 Hume Hwy.

**BALRANALD Caravan Park,** nr Sturt Hwy and Court St; 2 on-site vans; pets allowed.

**BARHAM Pioneer Caravan Park,** river frontage; 7 on-site vans; no pets.

**COROWA Caravan Park,** Deniliquin Rd; 2 on-site vans; pool; no pets.

**Ball Park,** on banks of Murray River; 6 cabin vans & 15 on-site vans; no pets.

**CULCAIRN Jubilee Park,** on Olympic Way; pets allowed.

**DENILIQUIN McLean Beach Caravan Park,** Butler St; 16 on-site vans; pets allowed.

**Mason's Paringa Caravan Park,** Ochertyre Street; 6 cabin vans & 12 on-site vans; pets allowed.

**Robin Hood Park,** Stevens Weir; check about pets and on-site vans.

**HUME WEIR Park,** on northern shore of reservoir (16km E of Albury); no pets.

**JERILDERIE Caravan Lodge,** 121 Jerilderie St; 2 on-site vans; pets allowed.

**MULWALA Hargreaves Caravan Park,** 27 Corowa Rd; 6 on-site vans; pets allowed.

**Cypress Gardens,** Melbourne Rd; 13 cabin vans & 20 on-site vans; no pets.

**Turtle Park;** check about vans and pets.

**TOCUMWAL Caravan Park,** cnr Burton St and Finley Rd; 10 on-site vans; pool; pets allowed.

**The Boomerang Way,** Newell Hwy; 3 cabin vans & 3 on-site vans; no dogs allowed.

## NEW ENGLAND DISTRICT

**BOURKE Bullamunta Tourist Park,** Mitchell Hwy; 6 on-site vans; pets allowed.

**Mitchell's Caravan Village,** Mitchell St; 9 on-site vans; pets allowed.

**COOLAH Cunningham Caravan Park,** Bruce St; pets allowed.

**MUDGEE Caravan Park,** end of Douro St; check pets and on-site vans.

**Lions Drive Caravan Park,** Sydney Rd; 6 on-site vans; pets allowed.

**Cooinda Caravan Park,** Bell St; check about pets and vans.

**TRANGIE Caravan Park,** Goan St; 4 on-site vans; pets allowed.

**Tandara Caravan Park,** John St; 5 cabin vans & 10 on-site vans; small pets allowed.

**WARREN Caravan Park,** Stafford St; 4 on-site vans; pets allowed.

**WELLINGTON Caves Caravan Park,** adjacent to Caves Road; bbq; playground; pool; no dogs.

**Ridgecrest Holiday Cottages.**

**Burrendong Dam;** Burrendong Dam Rd; 9 on-site vans; pets allowed.

## RIVERINA DISTRICT

**GUNDAGAI Caravan Village,** Junee Rd; 17 on-site vans; pets allowed.

**Gundagai River,** Middleton Dr, north bank of river; 4 on-site vans; pets allowed.

**HAY Caravan Park,** Sturt Hwy; 2 cabin vans; 6 on-site vans; pets allowed.

**NARRANDERA Lake Talbot Caravan Park,** 2 cabin vans; 6 on-site vans; pets allowed.

**Lake Talbot Lodge & Caravan Park,** Broad St; bbq; playground; pool; 2 cabin vans & 10 on-site vans; pets allowed.

**Transit Caravan Park,** junction Newell and Sturt Hwys, Gillenbah; 4 on-site vans; no pets.

**TUMUT Riverglade Caravan Park,** on river bank; 4 cabin vans & 15 on-site vans; pets allowed.

**Blowering Entrance,** Snowy Mountains Hwy; 11 on-site vans; pets allowed.

**WAGGA WAGGA Tourist Park,** Johnston St; 7 cabin vans & 23 on-site vans; no pets.

**Riverview Caravan Park,** Hammond Ave; 18 on-site vans; no pets.

**Forest Hill Caravan Park,** Sturt Hwy, Wagga Wagga East; 2 cabin vans & 20 on-site vans; pets allowed.

## SNOWY MOUNTAINS DISTRICT

The following are just a few examples of sites in this area – there are many others located around the lakes. Other forms of accommodation are also available – lodges, farms etc. A more detailed list can be obtained from the New South Wales Government Travel Centre.

**Buckenderra Holiday Centre,** 36 km W of Cooma, off Snowy Mountains Hwy on Berridale Rd; camping and caravan sites; 37 on-site vans; pets allowed under control.

**Anglers Reach,** 14 km NW of Adaminaby; camping and caravan sites; pets allowed under control.

**Braemar Bay Caravan Park,** North Eucumbene; camping and caravan sites; pets allowed under control.

**Lake Jindabyne Caravan Park,** Kosciusko Rd; 50 on-site vans; no pets.

**Snowline Caravan Park,** Kosciusko Rd; 3 km from Jindabyne; 16 cabin vans & 33 on-site vans; no pets.

# QUEENSLAND

## ATHERTON TABLELANDS

**HERBERTON Wild River Caravan Park,** Holdcroft Drive; on-site vans; kiosk and children's area; pets allowed.

**LAKE TINAROO Tinaburra Waters Lakeside Caravan Park,** via Tungaburra; cabins and 3 on-site vans; kiosk and children's play area; no dogs.

## BRISBANE

**ACACIA RIDGE Acacia Caravan Park,** 1691 Beaudesert Rd; on-site vans; kiosk and shopping nearby; children's area; swimming pool; no dogs allowed.

**BELMONT Belmont Garden Caravan Park,** Belmont Rd; on-site vans; kiosk and shopping nearby; children's play area; pets allowed.

**CAPALABA Greenacres Caravan Park,** cnr Mt Cotton and Greenfields Rds; 3 on-site vans; TV room; games room; shopping at park and nearby; children's area; pool; pets on application.

**CARINA Caravan Park,** Creek Rd; on-site vans; TV room; kiosk and shopping nearby; children's playground; pets allowed.

**EIGHT MILE PLAINS San Mateo Caravan Park,** 2481 Pacific Hwy; 4 on-site vans; shopping at park and locally; pool; no pets.

**HEMMANT Morris Marina,** 72 Aquarium Ave; kiosk; local shopping; children's play area; pets allowed.

**HOLLAND PARK Amaroo Gardens,** 771 Logan Rd; on-site vans; local shopping; no pets.

**WELLINGTON POINT Caravan Park,** Birkdale–Wellington Point Rd; on-site vans; kiosk; children's area; pets allowed.

**CAIRNS White Rock Cabins and Trailer Court,** Skull Rd and Bruce Hwy; on-site vans; TV room; games room; kiosk; children's area; pets allowed.

**Woree Caravan Park,** Bruce Hwy; cabins and 12 on-site vans; children's playground; kiosk; TV room; pool; pets allowed.

**Sunland Carapark Inn,** 49 Pease St; on-site vans; TV room; games room; children's area; kiosk; pool; pets allowed.

**Cool Waters Caravan Park,** Brinsmead Rd; on-site vans; TV room; games room; pool; kiosk; pets allowed.

**Freshwater Van Park,** 308 Kamerunga Rd, Freshwater; cabins; kiosk; games room; 20 on-site vans; pets allowed.

**Lake Placid Caravan Park,** Lake Placid; cabins and on-site vans; children's area; local shopping; pets allowed.

**CHARTERS TOWERS Mexican Caravan Park,** 75 Church St; cabins and 5 on-site vans; kiosk; pool; no pets.

**CLONCURRY Cloncurry Shire Council Caravan Park,** McIlwraith St; children's play area; nearby shopping; 6 on-site vans; pets allowed.

**COOKTOWN Cooktown Caravan Park,** Charlotte St; cabins and on-site vans; kiosk; check for pets.

**Peninsula Caravan Park,** Howard St; cabins and on-site vans; kiosk; children's area; pets allowed.

**Seaview Caravan Park,** Esplanade; on-site vans; local shopping; children's playground; pets allowed.

**CROYDON Golden Picdewehousma Caravan Park,** Brown St; (Croydon Shire Council); local shopping; bbq; some facilities; check for pets.

**DAINTREE Riverview Caravan Park;** 5 on-site vans; local shopping; no dogs.

**GATTON Lockyer Valley Caravan Park,** Warrego Hwy; on-site vans; children's play area; kiosk; pets allowed.

**Tent Hill Caravan Park,** Tent Hill via Gatton; on-site vans; children's area; kiosk; pets allowed.

**GEORGETOWN Georgetown Caravan Park,** Cemetery Rd (Etheridge Shire Council); 6 on-site vans; local shopping; pets allowed.

**GULF COUNTRY Burke and Wills Roadhouse,** Three Ways Rd Junction via Julia Creek (junction of Julia Creek/Normanton/Cloncurry Rds); electricity at van sites; kiosk; bbq; pets allowed.

**GYMPIE Gold Nugget Caravan Park,** 5 Bruce Hwy; cabins and 6 on-site vans; kiosk and local shopping; TV room; games room; children's play area; pets allowed.

**Gympie Caravan Park,** 1 Jane St; cabins and 13 on-site vans; TV room; local shopping; pets allowed.

**Rainbow Beach Caravan Park,** Rainbow Beach Rd, on-site vans; kiosk; children's area; pets allowed.

**Silver Fern Caravan Park,** Bruce Hwy, Kybong, 16km S of Gympie; 5 on-site vans; local shopping; children's area; pets allowed.

**INNISFAIL August Moon Caravan Park,** Bruce Hwy; 20 on-site vans; TV and games rooms; kiosk; children's area; pool; pets allowed.

**Bramston Beach Camping Ground,** Esplanade (Mulgrave Shire Council); some facilities; pets allowed.

**Flying Fish Point Camping Area,** Elizabeth St (Johnstone Shire Council); some facilities; pets allowed.

**Mango Tree Caravan Park,** 6 Couche St; 4 on-site vans; children's area; kiosk; pool; pets allowed.

**Plantation Village,** Evans Rd; cabins and on-site vans; games room; meals in restaurant; pets allowed.

**River Drive Caravan Park,** South Johnstone Rd; 2 cabin vans & 2 on-site vans; local shopping; TV room; pool; no dogs.

**MACKAY Central Caravan Park,** Malcomson St; North Mackay; cabins; children's play area; kiosk; pool; bbq; no dogs allowed.

**Hill Top Caravan Park,** 104 Evans Ave, North Mackay; 9 on-site vans; TV room; kiosk; bbq; no pets allowed.

**Tropical Caravan Park,** Bruce Hwy (6 km S of Mackay); cabins; 7 cabin vans & 12 on-site vans; children's area; kiosk; swimming pool; pets allowed.

**Mackay Beaches Caravan Park,** Petrie St, Far Beach; cabins; 4 cabin vans & 13 on-site vans; kiosk; children's area; pets allowed.

**Seawinds Caravan Park,** Blacks Beach; cabins and 6 on-site vans; kiosk; bbq; no dogs allowed.

**Halliday Bay Tourist Resort,** Halliday Bay; cabins; kiosk and local shopping; games room; bbq; restaurant nearby; pets on application.

**MARYBOROUGH City Caravan Park,** 125 Aldridge St; cabins and on-site vans; kiosk; washing and other facilities; no pets.

**Huntsville Caravan Park,** 23 Gympie Rd; cabins and 6 on-site vans; kiosk; children's playground; other amenities; pets allowed.

**Kelly's Roadhouse,** 148 Gympie Rd, cabins; kiosk; play centre/games room; pets allowed.

**Wallace Caravan Park,** 22 Ferry St; cabins and 12 on-site vans; local shopping; children's playground; no pets allowed.

**Boonooroo Fishermens Bend Caravan Park,** 5 on-site vans; TV room; play area for children; games room; pets allowed.

**Poona Poona Palms,** cabins and on-site vans; kiosk; playground; pets allowed.

**MOUNT ISA Mount Isa City Council Caravan Park,** 112 Marian St; kiosk; children's play area; other amenities; pets allowed.

**Riverside Caravan Park,** 195 Little West St; 6 on-site vans; local shopping; no dogs.

**Sunset Caravan Park,** 14 Sunset Dr; cabins and 5 on-site vans; games room; kiosk and children's playground; pets allowed.

**Argylle Caravan Park,** Cloncurry Rd; on-site vans; kiosk; play area; pets allowed.

**MUDGEERABA Mudgeeraba Caravan Park,** Springbrook Rd; on-site vans; games room; local shopping; children's area; pets allowed.

**NERANG Nerang Caravan Park,** Nerang St (on Nerang River); on-site vans; games room; kiosk and local shops; no pets.

**NOOSAVILLE All-A-Wah Caravan Park,** Mary St; 10 cabin vans; kiosk; children's play area; games room; pool; pets allowed.

**Noosa River Caravan Park,** Robert St; 4 cabin vans & 6 on-site vans; local shopping; children's area; pets allowed.

**Content Caravan Park,** 4 Weyba Rd; cabins; 5 cabin vans & 13 on-site vans; TV room; games room; local shopping; children's playground; pool; no pets allowed.

**ROCKHAMPTON Fitzroy Caravan Park,** Cowap St, North Rockhampton; cabins and on-site vans; games room and children's playground; pool; no dogs.

**Municipal Riverside Caravan Park,** Reaney St, North Rockhampton (Rockhampton City Council); some facilities; no pets.

**Southside Caravan Park,** Lower Dawson Rd; on-site vans; kiosk; pool; no pets.

**Cattle Country Caravan Park,** Bruce Hwy, Parkhurst; 6 cabin vans & 12 on-site vans; kiosk; children's area; pool; pets allowed.

**Country Club Caravan Park,** Bruce Hwy, North Rockhampton; 16 cabin vans; TV room; kiosk; children's area; pool; pets allowed.

**Ramblers Motel and Caravan Park,** Bruce Hwy; North Rockhampton; cabins and on-site vans; kiosk; children's playground; pool; no pets.

**SOMERSET DAM Somerset Dam Caravan Park** (Brisbane City Council); some facilities; pets allowed.

**TALLEBUDGERA CREEK Campdown Tally Valley Caravan Park,** Guineas Rd; on-site vans; TV; games rooms; kiosk; pets allowed.

**Tallebudgera Creek Camping Area,** Gold Coast Hwy (Gold Coast City Council); children's area; games room; local shopping; no pets.

**TOWNSVILLE Ross River Caravan Park,** Harvey Range Rd, Condon; on-site vans; local shopping; children's area; pets allowed.

**Rowes Bay Caravan Park,** Heatley Pde, Rowes Bay; 19 cabin vans; kiosk; children's playground; no pets.

**Walkabout Caravan Park,** cnr Bruce Hwy and University Rd; 10 on-site vans; kiosk; children's area; pool; no dogs allowed.

**Bohlevale Carapark,** 910 Ingham Rd; 24 on-site vans; kiosk; games room; pool; children's area; pets allowed.

**Inghams Tourist and Caravan Park,** Bruce Hwy; Ingham's cabins and 6 on-site vans; TV room; local shops; children's play area; pool; pets allowed.

**Ingham Municipal Caravan Park,** Townsville Rd; on-site vans; local shops; pets on application.

**Forrest Beach Caravan Park,** Allingham (16km E of Ingham); on-site vans; children's area; local shopping; pets allowed.

**Taylors Beach Caravan Park,** John Dory St; 6 on-site vans; kiosk; pool; pets allowed.

**Island Coast Caravan Park,** on beach front; 7 on-site vans; kiosk; children's play area; pool; pets allowed.

## SOUTH AUSTRALIA

**BARMERA Greenwood Caravan Park,** Queen Elizabeth Dr; powered/unpowered sites; pets allowed.

**BLANCHETOWN Scenic View Caravan Park,** Sturt Hwy; 3 on-site vans and cabins; powered sites; pets allowed.

**BERRI Riverside Caravan Park,** Riverside Ave, near PO; 6 cabin vans & 16 on-site vans; powered sites; pets allowed.

**GOOLWA River Murray Caravan Park,** near town centre on river bank; powered/unpowered sites; 4 on-site vans and cabins; pets allowed on leash.

**Hindmarsh Island Caravan Park,** Madsen St, Hindmarsh Island; powered/unpowered sites; 4 on-site vans and cabins; no pets.

**KINGSTON-ON-MURRAY Caravan Park,** 500m from PO; 6 cabin vans 13 on-site vans; powered/unpowered sites; pets allowed under control.

**LOXTON Riverfront Caravan Park,** Habels Bend, 3km from PO; 6 cabin vans & 6 on-site vans; sites available; no dogs.

**Showgrounds Caravan Park,** Pine Ave; powered/unpowered sites; pets allowed on leash.

**MANNUM Caravan Park,** near town centre next to ferry; 10 on-site vans and cabins; pets allowed.

**MENINGIE Lakeside Caravan Park,** near town centre on the shores of Lake Albert; powered/unpowered sites; 12 on-site vans and cabins; pets allowed.

**MILANG Milang Caravan Park,** situated on the shores of Lake Alexandrina; 10 on-site vans; powered/unpowered sites; pets allowed.

**MORGAN Riverside Caravan Park,** near town centre; cabins; 5 cabin vans & 7 on-site vans; powered/unpowered sites; pets allowed.

**MURRAY BRIDGE Avoca Dell,** east of town centre, over bridge on river bank; powered sites; on-site vans and cabins; pets allowed.

**Oval Caravan Park,** 4 Le Messurier St; 7 on-site vans and cabins; powered sites; no pets.

**Sturt Reserve,** on riverfront; powered/unpowered sites; pets allowed on leash.

**Wartz Princes Highway Caravan Park,** 5 km from PO on Adelaide Rd; 19 on-site vans and cabins; pets allowed.

**White Sands Holiday Resort,** Jervois Rd; powered/unpowered sites; 1 on-site van and cabins; pets allowed.

**PARINGA Caravan Park,** Sturt Hwy; 6 cabin vans & 9 on-site vans; powered sites; pets allowed except at Easter.

**SWAN REACH Caravan Park,** Victoria St; usual sites; on-site vans and cabins; pets allowed.

# TASMANIA

It is a fallacy to believe that so remote from civilisation are the lakes of Tasmania that no facilities exist within this rugged wilderness to cater for the angler who wishes to tread deeply into the very heart of it. That was true not so very long ago, but now the picture has changed. Many of the more widely publicised waters have facilities of some kind. They may only consist of a barbecue area or picnic site, but camping areas are also to be found in some cases — not necessarily with warm showers and washing machines (even having power available is a luxury in some parts), but they're suitable enough for you to be able to pitch a tent and cook a meal in the old-fashioned way over a kerosene or portable gas unit.

Among the better known waters that have camping sites of some description are **Arthurs Lake,** where areas for camping exist from Canal Bay to Tods Corner and Cramps Bay. **Penstock Lagoon** allows for camping around the lakeside from Canal Shore to Beginners Bay. **Lake St Clair** offers camping at Cynthia Bay, which is under the control of the National Parks and Wildlife Service.

On **Lake Pedder** we find many facilities, mostly basic picnic areas, some with toilet blocks, but at Edgar Dam there is a camping area, rather exposed and with limited amenities only. A similar place for camping is found at Scotts Peak. Both are at the southern end of the lake and also have boat ramps. Near the northern tip of Pedder at Teds Beach a public shelter is discovered, along with toilets and a boat launching area. At Strathgordon there is also a caravan park, but although more such parks are being added to the list already available from the tourist offices of Tasmania, generally they are a fair distance from the lakes, and as such are not a great deal of use to us, but that situation will change.

## CAMPERVAN-HIRE

The following is a limited list of companies specialising in campervan-hire. It is suggested that whenever possible arrangements for the hire of a vehicle be made well in advance, so that it can be waiting for your arrival by air or sea.

**Tourmobile Rentals** Hobart: 344 Tasman Hwy, Mornington; Launceston: Hobart Rd; Devenport: Paradise Sands Caravan Park, PO Box 185, Ulverstone. Offers most kinds of campervans from 3 to 9 berths, fully equipped; also minibuses for hire.

**Southern Cross Rentals** Hobart: 156 Harrington St; Launceston: 43 Brisbane St and Airport Rd; Devenport: 59 Formby Rd; Wynyard: 5 Inglis St. Campervans, motor homes, station wagons, caravans.

**Explorer Motor Caravans,** PO Box 26, Longford. 5-6–berth motor caravans, some with shower and toilet; package deal with Ansett.

**Motor Holidays** (Tas.), 97 Chapel St, Glenorchy. 4-, 5- or 6-berth vans; auto or manual drive; no charge for distance or extra person.

**Touring Motor Homes,** 8 Granville St, West Launceston. Has vans of 4, 6 and 8 berths, some with shower and toilet; package deal with airline.

**Dolphin Motor Caravan,** PO Box 47, Evandale. Super Apex rates available through Ansett.

**Tasmanian Mobile Motels,** PO Box 20, Launceston. Australia's largest Volkswagen Campmobile operator; bookings through TAA and Ansett or travel agent.

**El Centro Campervans,** 69 Wellington St, Launceston. Check for rates and types of vans.

# VICTORIA

## BRIGHT DISTRICT

**Alpine Cabins and Caravan Park,** Mountbatten Ave; powered/unpowered sites; 17 on-site vans, cabins; bookings necessary during all holidays; no pets.

**Bright Municipal Caravan Park,** Cherry Ave; powered/unpowered sites; 9 on-site vans; bookings necessary Christmas (minimum two weeks), Easter and school holidays; no dogs Xmas, January and Easter.

**Green Hill Caravan Park,** Harrietville Rd; powered/unpowered sites; 17 on-site vans; bookings necessary during most holidays; children's playground; bbq; pool; games room; pets allowed.

**Pine Valley Camping Park;** powered/unpowered sites; 6 cabin vans & 10 on-site vans; bookings necessary during holidays; washing facilities; no pets.

**Freeburgh Caravan Park,** Harrietville Rd; powered/unpowered sites; 7 on-site vans, 1 on-site flat; bookings necessary during holidays; children's playground and usual facilities; pets allowed.

**Riverside Park, Toorak Rd;** powered/unpowered sites; 3 on-site vans; 6 flats; bookings necessary at all times; bbq; children's playground; pets allowed in caravan park only.

## VICTORIAN WATERS

**ALEXANDRA Tourist Park,** William St, close to Goulburn River; powered/unpowered sites; on-site vans; bookings necessary Christmas, Easter; pets allowed.

**Twin Rivers Caravan Park,** Breakaway Rd (on bank of Goulburn River); 6 cabin vans & 6 on-site vans; usual sites; kiosk; playground; launching ramp; boat mooring; book early holiday season; no pets.

**Fraser National Park,** near Alexandra on Lake Eildon; no power but 200 sites; wildlife abounding in park.

**Riversdale Caravan Park,** Maroondah Hwy, between river and town; powered/unpowered sites; 6 on-site vans; pets allowed.

**BACCHUS MARSH Cherry Inn Caravan Park,** Stamford Hill, Old Ballarat Rd; usual sites with 4 on-site vans; service station; fruit stall; pets allowed.

**BAIRNSDALE Tourist Caravan Park,** Princes Hwy; powered/unpowered sites; 12 en-suite units; 36 cabin vans & 5 on-site vans; bookings necessary Christmas, Easter; pool; children's playground; fauna park with native animals; tennis court; TV lounge; washing facilities; recreation rooms and trampoline; no pets.

**Mitchell Gardens Caravan Park,** Princes Hwy; 4 cabin vans & 5 on-site vans; usual sites; bookings necessary holiday periods; no pets.

**Mitchell River Caratel and Camp Park,** Lindenow; 6 on-site vans; toilet, shower each van; usual sites; coin-operated washing machines, dryer; bbq; swings; pets allowed.

**Shady Trees Caravan Park,** Princes Hwy; powered/unpowered sites; 6 on-site vans; TV hire; children's area; bookings required Christmas, Easter; no pets.

**BALLARAT Welcome Stranger Caravan Park,** 263 Scott Pde, 0.5km from Eureka Stockade turn-off; usual sites; tents welcome; 19 cabin vans & 6 on-site vans (bedding needed on hire); 2 en-suite units; washing facilities; TV lounge; bbq; many other amenities; no dogs.

**Lake Wendouree Caravan Park,** Avoca Hwy, Gillies St (opposite lake); 25 on-site vans; usual sites on large pine forest; many other facilities; no pets.

**Shady Acres,** Melbourne Rd, on 'Kryal Castle' side of Ballarat; powered/unpowered sites; 12 cabin vans & 18 on-site vans; washing facilities; TV lounge; adventure playground; many other amenities; bookings preferred.

**BEMM RIVER Caravan Park,** powered/unpowered sites; 4 on-site cabins; children's playground; store nearby; bookings necessary holidays times; pets allowed.

**Alcheringa Lodge,** Sydenham Pde; powered/unpowered camping permitted; 7 cabins; all usual facilities; bookings necessary during holiday periods; pets allowed.

**Fellowes Caravan Park,** PO Box 484, Orbost, 8 powered sites; camping permitted; 7 on-site cabins; bbq; playground; bookings required during holidays periods; pets allowed.

**BONNIE DOON Caravan Park,** backwater of Lake Eildon; 6 cabin vans & 7 on-site vans; usual sites with camping allowed; washing facilities; children's playground; no pets.

**Lakeside Caravan Park,** Hutchinson's Rd; on-site vans, cabins; powered/unpowered sites; ramp; pool; recreation centre and other facilities; bookings necessary during holiday periods; no pets.

**Peppin Point Holiday Park,** Maintongoon Rd; usual sites plus 9 cabin vans & 9 on-site vans; horse riding and boat hire; boat ramp; fuel; golf course nearby; tennis courts; volleyball; table tennis; swimming; other amenities available, including laundry; bookings necessary holiday periods; no pets.

**CAMPERDOWN Town Caravan Park,** near Lake Bullen Merri; powered/unpowered sites; 3 on-site vans; usual facilities; bookings necessary Christmas, Easter, long weekends; pets allowed.

**Purrumbete Lake Camping/Caravan Park,** situated southern end of lake; usual sites and amenities with 2 cabin vans; boat launching and mooring.

**EDENHOPE Lake Wallace Caravan Park,** 22 Lake St; powered/unpowered sites (10 for tents); laundry; skiing; fishing; children's playground; bookings preferred Christmas, Easter; pets allowed by negotiation.

**EILDON Caravan Park,** Eildon Rd; powered/unpowered sites; camping; 8 cabin vans & 8 on-site vans (no linen or cutlery); laundry; kiosk; gas; tennis court; bbq; children's playground; bookings necessary most holidays; no pets.

**Goughs Bay Caravan Park,** bayside Boulevard, Goughs Bay; camping permitted; powered/unpowered sites; store; gas; children's playground; bookings necessary Christmas, Easter, long weekends; no pets.

**Kays Caravan Park,** Banumum Rd, Mansfield (Lake Eildon); usual sites with camping permitted; 16 on-site vans; 6 cabins; boat-launching ramps; houseboats; ski boats for hire; tennis court; horse riding; no pets.

**Jerusalem Caravan Park;** powered/unpowered sites; store; gas; laundry; bbq; Eildon pool; bookings necessary Christmas, Easter; pets allowed.

**EPPALOCK Caravan Park,** via Axedale; powered/unpowered sites; 10 executive en-suites; camping permitted; store; gas; open-air theatre December to January; boat ramp; bookings necessary December to April; no pets.

**Lakeshore Caravan Park,** adjacent weir wall; usual sites with camping allowed; on-site vans; mini-bike track; tennis court; recreation room; bbq; children's playground; bookings necessary Easter, long weekends; no pets.

**Metcalfe Pool Caravan Park,** on Lake Eppalock via Redesdale; 4 on-site vans; powered sites; laundry; store; gas; bookings necessary all holiday periods; no pets.

**Moorabee Lodge Caravan Park,** Derrinal Pool; 4 on-site vans; powered/unpowered sites; 10 tents; tennis and squash courts; boat ramp; children's playground; bookings required Easter and Christmas (two-week min); no pets.

**GEELONG Caravan Park,** Princes Hwy, Waurn Ponds; 8 on-site vans; plus usual powered sites; each with individual amenities; pool; children's playground; store; no pets.

**Riverglen Caravan Park,** Barrabool Rd; powered sites; 3 cabin vans & 35 on-site vans; bathroom and babies bath; modern laundry; bookings necessary at all times; no pets.

**Seabrae Caravan Park,** Clifton Ave, Leopold; powered sites; 9 on-site vans; boat launching ramp; tennis court; bookings necessary 18 December to 1 February (two weeks min.), Easter; no dogs.

**Eldorado Tourist Park,** Geelong–Ballarat Rd (Midland Hwy); 14 cabin vans & 6 on-site vans; 52 powered sites, all with own en-suite; opposite drive-in theatre; no dogs.

**GLENMAGGIE Camping Park,** Licola Rd; powered/unpowered sites; usual facilities with laundry; bbq; golf nearby; bookings necessary holiday periods; no pets.

**HALLS GAP Lakeside Caravan Park,** PO Box 4, Halls Gap; usual sites with 13 cabin vans & 9 on-site vans; 3 flats; amenities include store and gas; bookings necessary at all times; no pets.

**Lake Fyan's Caravan Park,** Pomonal via Stawell; 9 cabin vans & 9 on-site vans; camping and caravan sites; TV hire; bookings necessary for Christmas by August and Easter visits to be booked by February; no pets.

**Zumstein's Tourist Park,** Horsham Rd, Halls Gap; powered/unpowered sites; 100 tents; 4 on-site vans; bookings required all holiday seasons, no bookings taken at Easter; no pets.

**Grampians Gardens Caravan Park,** cnr Ararat and Stawell Rds; 4 cabin vans & 20 on-site vans; camping permitted; powered sites; 6 cabins; amenities include laundry; store; children's playground; recreation room; bbq; pool; bookings necessary all holidays; pets allowed.

**HEATHCOTE Queen Meadow Caravan Park,** Barrack St; camping permitted on powered/unpowered sites; 5 on-site vans; laundry; gas; children's area and recreation room; bookings necessary Christmas to Easter; pets allowed.

**HORSHAM Caravan Park,** Firebrace St; camping permitted on powered/unpowered sites; 12 on-site vans which require advance bookings; kiosk; gas; pets allowed.

**Wimmera Lakes Caravan Park,** Western Hwy; camping allowed on powered sites; 13 cabin vans & 4 on-site vans; facilities include laundry; ironing; kiosk; bbq; pool; pets allowed.

**JAMIESON Caravan Park;** normal sites; laundry; bbq; children's playground; bookings necessary all holidays; no pets.

**KERANG Caravan Park,** Riverland Drive; bookings not necessary excepting on-site vans at holiday periods; usual sites for vans and tents; children's playground; kiosk; gas; laundry; pets allowed.

**Ibis Caravan Park,** cnr Loddon and Murray Valley Hwy; 3 cabin vans & 10 on-site vans; powered/unpowered sites; washing facilities; children's playground; bookings necessary all holidays; pets allowed.

**KYNETON Caravan Park,** Clowes St; powered/unpowered sites; 20 tent sites; 3 on-site vans; children's playground; bbq; pool; bookings necessary Christmas, Easter; no pets.

**LAKE BOLAC Caravan Park,** Foreshore Rd, PO Box 73; 4 on-site vans; usual sites and amenities; including tennis; bowls; shop nearby; fishing; swimming; boating; water-skiing; bookings necessary at Easter; pets allowed.

**LAKE BURRUMBEET Caravan Park,** Western Hwy; 6 on-site vans; powered/unpowered sites; swimming; fishing; bookings necessary Christmas, Easter, long weekends; pets allowed.

**The Russel Reserve,** South Shore, Lake Burrumbeet; powered/unpowered sites; 34 tent sites; spring water taps all sites; store; gas; children's playground; 3 boat ramps; bbq; no dogs.

**MAFFRA Caravan Park,** Johnson St; 16 powered sites; 4 on-site vans; children's playground; pool; golf nearby; pets allowed.

**Mallacoota Camp Park,** Allan Dr; 8 on-site vans; powered/unpowered sites; playground; bbq; bookings necessary Christmas, Easter, May school holidays; pets allowed.

**Beachcomber Caravan Park,** Betka Rd; 12 on-site vans; 32 powered sites; bbq; children's playground; private jetty; bookings necessary most holidays; check concerning pets.

**Holiday Haven,** Maurice Ave; powered/unpowered sites; 5 cabins; 2 on-site vans; 2 self-contained flats; bookings required all holiday periods; check concerning pets.

**Mount Beauty Caravan Park,** Kiewa Valley Hwy; 10 on-site vans; 90 powered sites; 10 unpowered and tent sites; 12 motel units; bookings necessary most holidays; no pets.

**Mount Buffalo National Park;** camping ground open November to May; shelters; fireplaces available in the park; caravans permitted November to May; power not obtainable; walking fishing, summer and autumn; no pets.

**Nagambie Caravan Park,** 143 High St; powered/unpowered sites; 12 on-site vans; washing facilities; children's playground; kiosk; LPG; all-weather boat ramp; pets on application.

**Chinamans Bridge Camping Ground,** Vickers Rd; usual sites; washing facilities; boating and fishing nearby; boat launching ramp; bookings necessary holiday periods; no dogs.

**NEWSTEAD Welshmans Reef Caravan Park,** on shore of Cairn Curran Reservoir; 2 on-site vans; camping permitted at powered and unpowered sites; laundry; gas; bbq; children's playground; bookings necessary all holiday periods and long weekends; pets allowed.

**NICHOLSON River Caravan Park,** Princes Hwy, powered/unpowered sites; 5 on-site vans; tents allowed; usual amenities; bookings necessary Christmas, Easter, long weekends; no dogs.

**RUSHWORTH Waranga Basin Caravan Park;** camping on powered/unpowered sites; 7 on-site vans; children's bathroom; playground; kiosk; LPG; all weather boat ramp; bookings requested Christmas and Easter; no pets.

**SALE Caravan Park,** Princes Hwy; powered/unpowered sites, most sewered; 14 on-site vans arranged; camper kitchen; showers; laundry; bbq; no pets.

**Carinya Caravan Park,** 180 York St; powered sites; 7 cabins; 3 on-site vans (no linen or crockery); bookings necessary all holiday periods; pets allowed.

**Thomson River Caravan Park,** South Gippsland Hwy; 7 on-site vans; powered/unpowered sites; children's playground; bbq; laundry; camper kitchen; no pets.

**SWAN HILL Riverside Caravan Park,** Monash Drive; 12 cabin vans & 6 on-site vans; powered/unpowered sites; babies room; outside dish washing facilities; kiosk; gas; playground; bookings necessary all holiday periods; no pets.

**Pental Island Caravan Park Holiday Farm,** Pental Island Rd; 9 cabins; 6 cabin vans; powered/unpowered sites; camping; separate room with toilet and shower for handicapped people; all sporting facilities; bookings requested long weekends and school holidays; no pets.

**Pioneer City Park,** Murray Valley Hwy; 17 cabin vans & 25 on-site vans; powered/unpowered sites, sewered; kiosk; laundrette; LPG; bbq; playground; pets allowed.

**THORNTON Caravan Park,** Goulburn Valley Hwy; camping permitted; powered/unpowered sites; 5 cabins; laundry; gas; pool; bbq; fish farm adjoining park; booking necessary Christmas, Easter; pets allowed.

**WANGARATTA North Cedars Caravan Park;** 13 cabins; 3 cabin vans & 16 on-site vans; usual sites; store; gas; children's playground; TV hire; bookings necessary at all times; no pets.

**Painters Island Caravan Park,** Pinkerton Crescent; 2 on-site vans; powered/unpowered sites; facilities include store; gas; bbq; children's playground; adjacent pool; booking suggested for Christmas, School Holidays, long weekends; no pets.

**Regal Caravan Park,** Parfitt Rd; 20 on-site vans; 40 powered sites; 4 tents; store; gas; bbq; playground; bookings necessary all holiday periods; pets allowed.

**WARRNAMBOOL Foreshore Reserve;** two van parks – Surf Side One and Surf Side Two; 900 powered sites; laundrettes; kiosks; bbq; children's playground and other facilities; no pets allowed December to February.

**Caravan Lodge Caravan Park,** Henna St; powered sites; 2 cabin vans & 19 on-site vans; 3 flats; gas; store; pool; children's playground nearby; bookings necessary all holiday periods; no pets.

**Ocean Beach Caravan Park,** Pertobe Rd; powered sites; 10 tent sites; 16 cabin vans & 3 on-site vans; 12 separate amenities sites; store; gas; playground; recreation room; bbq; TV hire; booking necessary Christmas, Easter; No dogs.

**Flying Horse Inn,** Princes Hwy, Warrnambool East; powered/unpowered sites; camping permitted; 15 on-site vans; gas; store; take-away food; pool; playground; recreation room; bbq; booking requested Christmas, Easter; pets allowed.

**WINCHELSEA Yuringa Caravan Park,** Princes Hwy; powered/unpowered sites; tent sites; 2 on-site vans; laundry; playground; pets allowed.

**YAMBUK Lake Caravan Park;** powered/unpowered sites; 100 unpowered sites; ample room for camping; laundry; bbq; children's playground; booking necessary Christmas, Easter; pets allowed.

## WESTERN AUSTRALIA

**DERBY Caravan Park,** Rowan St; derby; 19 on-site vans available; pets allowed.

**WINDJANA GORGE NATIONAL PARK Camping Area;** located at the gorge; no power; no dogs.

**FITZROY CROSSING Inn Caravan Park,** adjacent to hotel; 2-3 berth cabins available; no cooking facilities; pets allowed.

**Geike Gorge National Park Camping Area,** located at gorge, 17 km N of Fitzroy Crossing township; apply ranger on-site; no power; no pets.

**HALLS CREEK Caravan Park,** cnr Roberta Ave and Bridge St; 9 on-site vans; pets allowed.

**WOLF CREEK CRATER** (Caranya Station) Camping Area; no fee; no pets.

**KUNUNURRA Lake Argyle Caravan Park,** Lake Argyle Tourist Village, PO Box 216 Kununurra; 2-man tents available; pets allowed.

**Coolibah Drive Caravan Park,** 2 km from town, Lot 1101, Coolibah Drive, Kununurra; pets allowed.

**Rigby's Caravan Park,** 3 km from town, Levee Bank Rd, PO Box 52, Kununurra; no on-site vans; camping allowed; no pets.

**Town Caravan Park,** Bloodwood Dr, Kununurra; no advance bookings; 3 on-site vans; no dogs.

**WYNDHAM Three Mile Caravan Park,** Baker St, Wyndham; no on-site vans; no advance bookings; no pets.

**The Gorge's Caravan Park,** located in town, 2nd Ave; on-site vans available; camping allowed; pets allowed.

**BRUNSWICK Caravan Park,** South-West Hwy, 0.5 km from town, beside river; apply to caretaker; camping sites offered; no advance bookings; dogs allowed on leash.

**MARGARET RIVER Caravan Park,** 36 Station Rd; 2 km from town, 10 km from beach; 10 on-site vans; pets allowed.

**Prevelly Park Holiday Resort,** PO Box 18, Margaret River; 10 on-site vans; camping allowed; no dogs.

**Riverview Caravan Park,** Wilmott Ave, Margaret River; 1 km from town, 10 km from beach; 7 on-site vans; camping sites; pets allowed.

**MUNDARING Caravan Park,** Great Eastern Hwy, Mahogany Creek; 25 km from Perth, 2 km west of Mundaring; no on-site vans; no pets.

**PEMBERTON Karri Caravan Park,** Jamieson St; Pemberton; pool available; no on-site vans; no pets.

# GOVERNMENT TOURIST BUREAUX

**AUSTRALIAN CAPITAL TERRITORY**
Northbourne Ave,
CANBERRA 2601
(062) 45 6464

64 Castlereagh St,
SYDNEY 2000
(02) 233 3666

102 Elizabeth St,
MELBOURNE 3000
(03) 654 5088

**NEW SOUTH WALES**
140 Phillip St,
SYDNEY 2000
(02) 23 7100

16 Spring St,
SYDNEY 2000
(02) 231 4444

Cnr Queen & George St,
BRISBANE 4000
(07) 229 8833

45 King William St,
ADELAIDE 5000
(08) 231 3167

**QUEENSLAND**
196 Adelaide St,
BRISBANE 4000
(07) 833 5255

75 Castlereagh St,
SYDNEY 2000
(02) 232 1788

257 Collins St,
MELBOURNE 3000
(03) 654 3866

25 Gareema Pl,
CANBERRA 2601
(062) 48 8411

10 Grenfell St,
ADELAIDE 5000
(08) 212 2399

55 St. Georges Tce,
PERTH 6000
(09) 325 1600

**SOUTH AUSTRALIA**
18 King William St,
ADELAIDE 5000
(08) 212 1505

143 King St,
SYDNEY 2000
(02) 232 8388

25 Elizabeth St,
MELBOURNE 3000
(03) 614 6522

**TASMANIA**
80 Elizabeth St,
HOBART 7000
(002) 30 0211

149 King St,
SYDNEY 2000
(02) 233 2500

256 Collins St,
MELBOURNE 3000
(03) 653 7999

32 King William St,
ADELAIDE 5000
(08) 211 7411

217-219 Queen St,
BRISBANE 4000
(07) 221 2744

5 Canberra Saving's Centre
City Walk
CANBERRA 2600
(062) 47 0888

100 William St
PERTH 6000
(09) 321 2633

**VICTORIA**
230 Collins St,
MELBOURNE 3000
(03) 619 9444

61 Market St,
SYDNEY 2000
(02) 233 5499

16 Grenfell St,
ADELAIDE 5000
(08) 231 4129

221 Queen St,
BRISBANE 4000
(07) 221 4300

**WESTERN AUSTRALIA**
722 Hay St,
PERTH 6000
(09) 322 2999

92 Pitt St,
SYDNEY 2000
(02) 233 4400

35 Elizabeth St,
MELBOURNE 3000
(03) 614 6833

Cnr. Grenfell & King William Sts,
ADELAIDE 5000
(08) 212 1344

243 Edward St
BRISBANE 4000
(07) 229 5794

**NORTHERN TERRITORY**
31 Smith St. Mall,
DARWIN 0800
(089) 81 6611

345 George St,
SYDNEY 2000
(02) 262 3744

415 Bourke St,
MELBOURNE 3000
(03) 670 5007

48 Queen St,
BRISBANE 4000
(07) 229 5799

9 Hindley St,
ADELAIDE 5000
(08) 212 1133

799 Hay St,
PERTH 6000
(09) 322 4255

121

# INDEX TO
# FRESHWATER FISHING AREAS AND
# TOURIST ATTRACTIONS